Trot On

Trot On

'frank, funny, sometimes tragic'

another little piglet in the popular
Sell the Pig series of travel memoirs

LIVRES
LEMAS

Tottie Limejuice

Published by LEMAS LIVRES
www.tottielimejuice.com

© Copyright L.M.K. Tither 2019
Cover design DMR Creative
Cover photo Neil Smith

TROT ON

ISBN 978-2-901-77317-7

Contents

To good friends

always there when you need them most

About the Author

Tottie Limejuice is the pen name of former journalist and freelance copywriter, Lesley Tither. Lesley also writes crime fiction as L M Krier and children's fiction as L M Kay.

Contact Details

If you would like to get in touch, please do so at:

tottielimejuice@gmail.com

facebook.com/LMKrier

facebook.com/groups/1450797141836111/

https://twitter.com/tottielimejuice

http://tottielimejuice.com/

Acknowledgements

I would just like to thank the people who have helped me with the Sell the Pig series:

Beta readers: Jill Pennington, Kate Pill, Jill Evans, Alison Sabedoria, Emma Heath, Margaret Russell

More from the same author

If you've enjoyed this book why not try more from author Lesley Tither under her different pen-names?

Writing travel memoirs/humour as Tottie Limejuice:

Sell the Pig
Is That Billinge Lump?
Mother Was It Worth It?
Biff the Useless Mention
Angling Bumateurs
Maman, vends le cochon

No Girl on This Train
Hobbit House in Italy

Writing crime fiction as L M Krier:

The First Time Ever
Baby's Got Blue Eyes
Two Little Boys
When I'm Old and Grey
Shut Up and Drive
Only the Lonely
Wild Thing
Walk on By
Preacher Man

Writing children's fiction as L M Kay:

The Dog with the Golden Eyes

Chapter One

The Scarlet Woman

'And trot on! Working trot, rising. That's great. Change the rein where you can, then give me a bit of canter on each leg.

'Good.

'Now just come back to walk and turn in and we'll talk about what will need working on before the exam.'

The customer I was talking to had booked a private one-hour assessment session with me at my riding centre in West Wales. She was planning on taking the British Horse Society Stage Two riding examination. Which meant that she'd already passed her Stage One at some point previously. I couldn't begin to imagine how, from what I'd just seen.

But I believe in teaching by encouragement. Various teachers I'd encountered through my school years had tried the old 'if you don't apply yourself harder, you'll never pass your (insert subject of choice) exam' ploy.

Such methods had never worked on me, so I didn't inflict them on others.

My motto was always start with the positive, with praise. Then slip in all the things which would need hard work and dedication to reach the required standard. Finally, return to the positive with more words of encouragement.

You know. A sh*t sandwich. With the hard to stomach bits in the middle.

Theoretically, I knew about such things as BHS exam

preparation. If pressed, I could wave a BHS Intermediate Teaching certificate, amongst others, which allowed me to train students up to Stage Three. Not to mention the famous 'Anceybum' – an Advanced National Certificate in Equine Business Management.

Impressive, eh?

I walked forward to talk to the rider, who had now brought the horse to a halt and was allowing it to relax and stretch a bit on a loose rein. The mare was called Independence Day Missed because, yes, you guessed it, she was born on the fifth of July. Not my horse, not my choice of name, and far too much of a mouthful for everyday use, so she was always known as Beastie, short for Wee Beast.

The rider was looking at me, eagerly, expectantly. Sure that she'd done a brilliant job and I would pronounce her well up to the requisite level, advising her to put in for the exam on the next available date.

'Be nice, Tottie. Focus on the positive,' the kind voice in my head was saying.

'What bloody positive?' the realistic voice in my head replied.

Returning the smile of my eager customer, I began with, 'I do love the cut of your hacking jacket. Is it a Harry Hall? It gives you such a good outline. Great for exam wear.'

The not so nice part of my diatribe took considerably longer to deliver. I sugar-coated it as best I could, making a long list of suggestions as to how the woman could work towards her stated goal.

I was far too kind to suggest giving up riding altogether and settling for knitting.

She was going to need a lot of tuition and I wouldn't even be getting the benefit of charging her for it. She wasn't from the area. She was in Wales on holiday and had been delighted to discover there was a BHS approved riding centre a thousand feet up a windswept plateau in the middle of nowhere, near to her chosen destination. So she'd booked an assessment lesson.

After I'd finished my delivery and we'd gone back to the yard, she went on her way happily with my list of suggestions. The fees for a long series of private lessons would have been a welcome source of income for me during the quiet season outside the main holiday period. But although I'm an eternal optimist, I didn't envy the instructor who took on the task of putting so many faults right.

I waved at her departing vehicle as it bumped and bounced its way up the several hundred yards of rough track across common grazing land from my riding centre up to the road. Then I untacked Beastie, gave her a quick brush-over, picked her feet out and turned her out with the others. They had a few hundred acres to graze on and she raced off with a joyful buck to find the rest of her herd.

So what was I doing here, living alone, most of the time, apart from around twenty horses to care for, plus some dogs and a couple of cats, on top of Llanllwni Mountain?

Well, it's a long story. And it involves me having to confess to you my time as a scarlet woman.

You may want to put the kettle on.

Sometimes in life, you realise you're making a huge mistake. But somehow you get caught up in the stream of things and you can't seem to find your way back to the riverbank to get out. Especially if you can't swim. Especially not against the current.

My marriage was a bit like that.

I'd always been adamant that I would never get married. As I never wanted children, not remotely, there didn't seem a lot of point.

Just a brief potted biography here, for those who've not yet read the Sell the Pig series. Or who've read it and forgotten.

I was born in Nantwich, Cheshire in the early 1950s, father a newspaper editor and district manager, mother a housewife, one brother, four years older. After a brief move to Preston, we settled, as a family, in Stockport, which was then in Cheshire, now in Greater Manchester, where I went to school – occasionally.

I was never particularly fond of my father and had no deliberate intention of following him into journalism. But writing was always my thing. Reading, and writing stories. So it was inevitable – pre-ordained, you could almost say - that journalism was where I would finish up.

I'd been passionately in love with horses ever since the early days of watching cowboys on television. I loved them all. *Wagon Train*, *The Range Rider*, *Champion the Wonder Horse*, *Bonanza*. I couldn't wait to be allowed to go for my first riding lesson.

Offerton, the leafy suburb where we lived, boasted a riding school which was situated at Halliday Hill Farm, on Holiday Lane. A listed building and a famous one, as it was the ancestral home of the Dodge Family who emigrated to America and founded Dodge City.

From the minute I walked up the steep stony drive, clutching my mother's hand, and caught the first ammonia waft of the muck heap, I was excited and terrified in equal measure. Emotions which stayed with me for my first lesson, being led round on a feisty little show-pony called Halliday My Word, or Redskin to her friends.

Holiday Lane was to become my second home. My preferred one. I was often to be found there when I should have been at school. When I was old enough, I worked there, evenings and weekends. Long hours, hard work, low pay. But the endless joys of riding for free. I'd have done it for no money, just the opportunity to inhale the intoxicating aroma of horse. It really is a powerful mood-altering drug which becomes an addiction, in a good way.

Even as a teenager, although never mercenary, I knew that the idea of a career with horses was never going to provide me with any sort of reasonable income. Not back in those days. Journalism, on the other hand, would give me a wage which would make me, if not rich, then at least able to carry on indulging my passion.

So after school, which I disliked intensely, I went to do a one-year pre-entry training course in Practical Journalism at Harris College, Preston. The course would be followed by a three-and-a-half year indenture period with a local newspaper.

Being in digs in Preston during the week in term-time meant I could go back to the family home every weekend and back to Holiday Lane, my spiritual home.

I wasn't remotely interested in university, or gap years or any of that malarkey. I was simply keen to get a qualification in order to go out into the big wide world to start earning money, and independence, as soon as I could. Clearly, marriage didn't figure on that agenda.

As part of our course, we had to find a subject on which to write an in-depth feature. Preston has a military connection and the digs where I was lodging, in Watling Street Road, were not far from Fulwood Barracks, then home to the Queen's Lancashire Regiment. I decided to do my piece on what motivated young men to join the Army, especially at a time which could see them serving and risking their lives at the height of the Northern Ireland troubles.

We had to run our ideas past our course tutor, an ex-RAF type complete with stiff moustache, who inevitably went under the nickname of Bomber. He cautioned me against turning it into a recruiting piece. But inevitably I would need to find out all about the recruitment process in order to write any kind of informed article. So my first port of call was to be a trip to the Armed Forces Recruiting Office in Preston's Fishergate.

At the time, I hung round with two friends and fellow students, Kay and Margaret, always known as Argy. They shared digs, I was on my own at mine. Most days we would buy bread and cheese then go back to their place to make

Welsh rarebit for our lunch. It was about all we could afford as impoverished students.

There was a third lodger at their house, a rather strange man with the most breathtaking body odour issues imaginable. He sought, unsuccessfully, to mask the problem with Old Spice aftershave. To this day, I can't abide the smell of it.

Kay and I would sometimes go out on our various assignments together. I would say for moral support, although that was not always the case.

But she was with me on the occasion when I first set foot into the strange and rather secretive world of the military, in that insignificant-looking recruiting office.

Which, you could say, is where it all began. And where it all started to go wrong.

Chapter Two
Right and Glory

I didn't know a great deal about the Armed Forces. I remembered an older cousin doing a short service commission in the Army at one point, and my uncle had been in the Royal Navy for a time, but that was about it.

I vaguely knew about ranks so assumed that the man behind the desk, who was watching as Kay and I walked in, was a corporal of some sort as he was sporting two stripes. I didn't yet know about the plethora of different regiments and their individual peculiarities. Only that my uncle, a Crown Court judge, had worn jodhpurs in his wartime service as a major in a cavalry regiment.

There were various posters about the place, one showing some sort of regimental emblem involving a canon or something similar. So perhaps something to do with artillery, I thought. It had a regimental motto above and below it.

'Ubique Quo Fas Et Gloria Ducunt' it proclaimed proudly. Mercifully, I had done enough Latin at school to read it with a straight face. The preferred translation in the context is 'Everywhere That Right And Glory Lead'.

The two-striper behind the desk asked us, helpfully enough, what he could do for us. Helpful, but he didn't sound too hopeful. He probably didn't get all that many young women walking in off the street asking about joining up, although it was something I had briefly considered in my sixth form days.

And clearly we were both far too young to have sons wanting to serve.

This was still in the days when women served in an entirely separate arm of the forces to men, the Women's Royal Army Corps. They didn't get to do any of the fun bits, certainly not front-line active service as they do now.

I launched in my pre-prepared *spiel* about my piece for college. Two-stripes started collecting up brochures and leaflets for me.

At that moment, the outer door opened and someone else came in. He had a couple of pips on his shoulders so he must have been an officer as Two-stripes addressed him as sir. Two-stripes explained to him what we were doing there, but two college students were clearly unimportant to an officer as he greeted us politely enough then carried on through a door at the back of the office and up some stairs, by the sound of it. To do more urgent officer-type things, no doubt.

Two-stripes made some sensible suggestions, including helping to arrange for me to visit Fulwood Barracks to talk to some real baby soldiers in the making.

We soon heard footsteps on the stairs again then a voice, rather a plummy one, resounded almost before the door opened, asking, 'Have those two birds gone yet, Bomb?'

Neither of us much cared for being referred to as birds by someone we didn't know. And Bomb? What kind of a weird name was that? I only discovered later on that the Royal Regiment of Artillery doesn't have corporals, they're called Bombardiers, hence Bomb for short. Just as in the Household Cavalry, those protectors of the Royals, they have the rank of Corporal of Horse instead of Sergeant as the root of that word is too similar to servant and they were traditionally recruited from the nobility, back in the day.

Now the word 'bird', especially in the north of England, uttered between females, is a term of endearment. Kay and I might well call one another 'bird' in everyday conversation. To have it uttered by an unknown male about us was less than complimentary.

But when the officer came through the door and saw us still standing there, he looked so mortified that even my hackles went back down as he stumbled a fulsome apology.

I hadn't taken much notice of him the first time he'd gone past us, but I now inspected him more closely.

He was short, definitely a few pounds overweight. Chubby, I thought to myself. Nicknames were a thing in my family. When my brother later met him for the first time, he secretly christened him Fatman, the name used for Billy Bunter in the books by his 'chums'. Two-pips also had a broken nose which was flatter than it should have been. A legacy, I later discovered, from the rugby field, where he played hooker. But his face was smooth, open and eager, with something of an endearing quality about it. Kay later pronounced him as looking like a bushbaby.

A friend, years later, who saw the wedding photos, said he looked like Manuel, the Spanish waiter, out of Fawlty Towers, although he didn't have a moustache when I first met him. *Fawlty Towers* wasn't on the TV at the time, either. We just had John Cleese in *Monty Python's Flying Circus. Fawlty Towers (Fatty Owls)* came later. I have to concede I can now see the resemblance, with hindsight.

In his haste to make amends, Two-pips finished up by asking us both out for a drink, together with 'Bomb'. We accepted, then spent the walk back to our college debating who fancied whom.

Kay was adamant that the lieutenant, as we discovered he was, fancied me. I thought he fancied her. We both decided that poor Bomb was just included as a chaperone. We decided that neither of us fancied either of them. Especially as Kay had a steady long-term boyfriend at home.

But we were impecunious students, living on next to nothing. A half a cider in the nearby Lamb and Packet was about our limit, with the occasional shared packet of pork scratchings. So why not an evening out mixing with some different types?

And it was certainly different, as first dates go. They turned up to collect us in a canvas-topped Army Land Rover. Not the most comfortable of carriages, as there wasn't room in the front for both of us. Bomb drove, the lieutenant, whose name, we discovered, was John, sat in the back occasionally grinning inanely from one to another of us.

It was hardly love at first sight. As the evening wore on, it became clear that it was me Fatman was interested in. Did I detect a slight sigh of relief from Kay that she was not the chosen one?

It was also clear that, although he thought himself a bit of a comedian, the lieutenant was more of a clown. The harder he tried, the more rubbish he spouted.

But he was persistent.

It wasn't long after our joint night out before he phoned me at my digs, having asked for the number, to invite me out again. This time just the two of us.

The earth didn't move. Angels didn't sing. There was no zing-boom. We just had a pleasant enough evening. So we started seeing one another. Going out together.

I'd had a few boyfriends. Nothing serious. Most of my spare time had always been spent up at the stables with the horses.

You're all going to expect me to explain how it happened. How I ended up marrying this man. I know. I'm a wordsmith, right? It should be easy to give you a reason that makes sense. But the more I think back on it, the more I find it difficult to explain it to myself, let alone to you.

I have only one word to offer up in my defence, Your Honour.

Alcohol.

A lot of our early courting took place at Army functions,

where the liquor flowed freely. We went to dinner nights in officers' messes, balls in Chester Castles, all sorts of glamorous occasions. And there was always plenty of champagne flowing, good wine with every course, port to follow for the loyal toast.

Somehow, it made it all seem better than it was.

Funnily enough, when I packed my bags for my weeks at college, full-length ball gowns were not high on the dress code for student wear.

Luckily for me, my mother and I were more or less the same size and she was always off out to glamorous occasions herself, accompanying my newspaper editor and film/food critic father.

Drinks parties at embassies, film premières, nights at the opera and the ballet. Weekends away with the Guild of British Newspaper editors of which my father was a member and was later to serve as national president. So she was certainly not short of frocks.

Added to that, her elder sister, my Auntie Ethel, was a professional seamstress who could run up any creation in the wink of an eye. The younger sister, Doris the not-so-dizzy blonde, the judge's wife, was also always gadding off to functions, dressed top to toe by Ethel. So all I ever had to do was to get the lieutenant to run me back to Stockport in his Triumph Herald and in two shakes I could trade my jeans and Snoopy T-shirt for some glamorous creation or another so I should go to the ball, Cinderella.

We used to joke that Mother's wardrobe was like the grandfather's chest in the old folk song, *'O Soldier, soldier, won't you marry me?'*

O soldier, soldier, won't you marry me
With your musket fife and drum?
O no sweet maid I cannot marry you
For I have no coat to put on.

So up she went to her grandfather's chest
And she got him a coat of the very, very best
And the soldier put it on.

The grandfather's chest could always provide the perfect item of clothing, just as my mother's wardrobe could.

None of it ever interested me in the slightest. I've never been into fashions, never been remotely girlie in that respect. It was just the required dress code for the events I went to. I was lucky that my landlady, Beryl, was kind enough always to do my hair for me when I was going out somewhere special so I generally managed to look presentable.

That first Christmas of seeing one another, I was invited down to Surrey to stay with his parents. I should have seen that as a warning sign. Particularly so when I was introduced to the brother-in-law, a goldsmith and jeweller who could, I was told, make a perfect engagement ring.

The father was a bank manager and they had a reasonable-sized detached house where they lived with the younger daughter, who was away at boarding school but was home for the holidays. The older sister was already married, with a child. The younger one made an art form of being a spoiled brat. When I retired to the guest bedroom the first night, I discovered she'd prepared the boarding-school favourite, an apple pie bed, complete with wet flannel inside it, for me.

I seemed to be met with approval, despite me not being conventional potential Army wife material, as when we were leaving to head back north, I got a kiss on the cheek from the father who apparently said to him after I left that I was 'the one'.

The lieutenant had already been to my home several times and had, for reasons which again remain unclear, been warmly accepted as acceptable boyfriend material by my parents.

The first time he'd been invited for a meal – Sunday lunch, as I recall – Mother had pulled out all the stops and brought out the best china. He was, as usual, playing the clown, telling some story he thought was amusing, accompanied by much waving of arms.

Unfortunately, he chose to do so just as Mother was bringing a vegetable tureen to the table. A flying backhander caught it, sending it flying and scattering peas all over the carpet.

I distinctly remember sitting there thinking what a complete idiot he was. Even through the blur of good wine, which was numbing things somewhat.

So why did I finish up marrying him?

Chapter Three
World Without End

For the year I spent at college in Preston, I was living something of a double life. By day, a moderately diligent student, studying such fascinating topics as Practical Journalism, Applied Law for Journalists, Public Administration, Typewriting, which I could already do well to a reasonable speed, and Teeline shorthand.

I'd done two years on a block release course at Stockport Technical College, whilst in sixth form at Stockport High School for Girls, learning Pitman, the classic shorthand. Pitman is an excellent shorthand, capable of being written at high speeds, ideal for anyone who needs to take down anything detailed and verbatim. It was the shorthand of choice for secretaries and old-school journalists. My father wrote it well, at good speeds.

The problem with it is that it is based on a series of symbols and short-forms. You can get dictionaries for it, of course, but if you don't happen to have a dictionary with you and you've forgotten a particular short-form, you can't read your notes back. Not a lot of use if you have a deadline to meet. Especially if you have a grumpy, drunken boss like my first one.

His real name was Maurice Brown – a name any readers of my Ted Darling crime series will know well. But he was always known in the office as Pissquick, for obvious reasons.

He was basically a nice man, capable of great kindness. But once he was the wrong side of several pints of mild, which he always interspersed with shots of gin, he turned into a monster. So it was never a good idea to be running too close to a deadline when he was waiting to put the paper to bed.

I can't think of any reason why I would ever use it in any shorthand I might take down, but, as an example, I seem to remember the short-form for 'world without end, amen', is a circle with a dot inside it. Imagine peering at that once you'd consumed rather too many glasses of wine at a reception, trying to figure out what the devil it meant.

I can remember leaving one such reception, on board a flagship of some container company in the Port of Manchester, so well oiled that I got the wheels of my little moped stuck in the tramlines around the docks and took a scenic route indeed to get back out to the road. I was well beyond the point of thinking rationally enough simply to stop, lift the moped out of the tracks, then continue on the tarmac.

So the National Council for the Training of Journalists, of which my father was a board member, although I always denied being related to him, decreed in its wisdom that journalists would adopt the much simpler shorthand, Teeline. It was quite new and innovative, having only been introduced in 1968.

Its simplicity lies in removing unnecessary letters from words and making the letters themselves faster to write, so it's quick to learn. You reach reasonable speeds much more quickly than with Pitman, although its top speeds are slower. There are no specific short-forms to learn, unless you create your own, so it's much easier to transcribe. You can read back a few letters and the context of the rest of it will tell you what the word is meant to be.

By the end of the first term, even the slowest of us was reasonably proficient at taking dictation and rendering it back into something resembling the original. It was not always easy because of the lecturer who often took us for dictation practice, who went under the nickname of Captain Bird's Eye because he looked like the bearded mariner of the adverts. He had an unfortunate speech impediment. This meant he always pronounced people as 'peetle'. And when you're concentrating on the word rather than the meaning, you do sometimes take it down phonetically.

Another of our lecturers had a pronunciation peculiarity. Our law lecturer was Irish, so he always pronounced 'films' as 'fillums'. In the typical way of students, we would all try to steer the conversation in such a way that he needed to say 'fillums'. The easiest way was to get him on to case law for defamation, with the famous case of Youssoupoff v MGM Pictures, which he always obligingly said as 'MGM Fillums'.

Ah, the small things which will amuse a student's brain by providing a distraction from doing any form of serous work.

But, as usual, I digress. Those were my days in college as a student. The wildest bit of excitement might be a cider and some pork scratchings in a pub, or round to someone's digs to sing a few folk songs. Fellow student Roy played the mandolin and patiently on one occasion showed me how to play the opening bars of Harvest Home. I could probably still do it if handed a mandolin.

In the evenings, mercifully usually at the weekend, or I would have been fit for nothing the next day, certainly not studying, I'd don the posh frocks and ball gowns and cross the portal into the totally different world of military functions at officer level. It sometimes felt like stepping back into an earlier era.

First there were the officers' uniforms. I'd naively thought, as the word was uniform, that they would all be the same. But no. Each regiment had its own dress uniform, with its own peculiarities. A lot of them, including the Artillery, required officers to wear rowelled spurs. If you were lucky, they remembered to take them off before asking you to dance.

I wasn't much of a dancer. Despite having done ballet for a few years and having a few certificates from the Royal Academy of Dance. Not the ballroom stuff which was all the rage in such settings. I could just about manage a St Bernard's Waltz, which we'd learned at school. Or a slow, where all that was required was to slump passively and hope the person who'd asked you up to dance could slide about without any catastrophic collisions with other dancers. Or I could manage a bit of a bop in the disco which was inevitably provided in another room. In the dark and with the strobe lights going, no one could actually see what you were doing anyway so it didn't matter.

Most of these functions were on days when I didn't have to get up early the following morning to go to college. Which was just as well, as they often went on late into the night, sometimes even to the following day.

'Carriages at midnight' was a fairly moderate affair. Sometimes breakfast was served at some ungodly hour of the morning, usually around four, then it was 'carriages at six'. Which would explain why, if they fell on a weekday, or if we'd had a hectic weekend of it, I could often be found at lunchtime on a college day, stretched out across several desks pushed together in one of our Journalism lecture rooms, fast asleep.

In between all the gallivanting, The Lieutenant and I were gradually taking one another round all the various relatives to be met, inspected and approved. Because somehow, at some moment I honestly don't remember, I had apparently agreed to us getting engaged.

I can't recount any romantic tales of a candlelit supper, him down on one knee, or any of that old malarkey. I must truly have been the wrong side of several vodka and limes because I honestly can't remember anything about it. But clearly it must have happened at some point as my mother and my Auntie Ethel were going into overdrive planning my dress, the bridesmaids' dresses and the cake, which my clever auntie could also make. Meanwhile father was seeking out the perfect venue for what would be something of a minor society wedding.

My intended had, of course, to be presented to my grandmothers on each side of the family. My mother's mother and my father's formidable surviving parent, both widowed. The latter was a farmer's daughter from a small village in Luxembourg. A very strong-minded lady who had made the journey to England when she was no more than a girl to work as what she called a children's nurse but would now be called a nanny for a wealthy family in Liverpool.

Granny was then fluent in four languages. Her own native Luxembourgish was not a lot of use internationally as it's mostly only spoken in one small country. But she also spoke French, German and Italian. It was fashionable in those days for children to be brought up speaking different languages so she was a prize catch.

Once settled in England, she quickly added English and, just for good measure, Esperanto, to her repertoire, although her English was always heavily accented with what sounded like a German accent. Sometimes her sentence construction was not typically English, which gave my brother and me some amusing moments, growing up.

She had a particularly bizarre habit of not addressing people directly, instead asking whatever her question was of someone else who was present. Hence if my brother or I spoke indistinctly, which of course we did frequently, just to hear her response, she would look to our mother and ask, in her accent, 'Vot does de child say?'

So it should have come as no surprise that after I had introduced my intended-although-I-still-had-no-idea-how-or-why and explained his military career, she turned to me to ask, 'But does he live in a barrack?'

But enough of all that old twaddle, I hear you say. All very interesting but, the burning question is, what about the sex? We were only just emerging from the Swinging Sixties, after all, so was there much swinging going on? From the light fittings? Had the ground started to move by now?

Well, first off, in our circumstances, it was not always easy to find the opportunity. I was in digs and my landlady, although happy for me to have my gentleman friend come a-calling, drew the line at any such visits being in my room. And you can forget immediately about the notion of trying anything frisky in a very draughty canvas-topped Army Land-Rover which was our usual mode of transport.

Whenever The Intended visited me at my extremely Victorian parents' home, he was given my room while I had a camp bed in my parents' room. One of those folding things which take a particular skill and a certain amount of agility to get into. On more than one occasion, after a night of merry-making in the mess, I managed to get it wrong and ended up folded inside the closed bed like one of those electric sandwich toasters.

It was much the same visiting his parents. Separate rooms at opposite ends of the house, with a creaky landing floor in between and parents who seemed to take it in turns to stay awake to make sure there was no hanky-panky going on under their roof.

On one memorable occasion visiting his aunt and uncle and their several children in wildest Devon, we were actually starting to get somewhere when the door to the guest room I was occupying suddenly opened wide on a small nephew looking forlorn and wanting a cuddle.

There certainly wasn't much chance to 'try before you buy' and I was inclined to put the fairly disastrous attempts down to the nerves brought on by such stolen moments.

Chapter Four

When I Was Bound Apprentice

As the end of our college course approached, we were all busily sorting ourselves out with somewhere to work at the end of it. In those halcyon days of the early 70s, it was relatively easy to walk into a job in journalism, especially waving an NCTJ proficiency certificate.

Some of the students already had jobs to go to, their places on the course having been sponsored by their employers. As far as I recall, with my fading memory, everyone found somewhere to go to on leaving. The next step on the qualification route was to be indentured (apprenticed) to a newspaper for three years.

Any folkies reading this (folk music lovers) will immediately get the reference of this chapter title. The least little thing gives me an earworm, a song which springs to my mind and stays there. The song The Lincolnshire Poacher, which we learned at junior school, beings, 'When I was bound apprentice in famous Lincolnshire.'

Most of us had passed our course exams, or almost all of them. A sprained wrist in a riding accident had meant I'd failed my shorthand test so would have to sit that again. I could write and read it back well enough to operate in the workplace in the meantime, as long as I didn't keep injuring myself.

I wasn't planning on moving away from home just yet. The Intended (why? I still don't know. Perhaps by the end of this book you might be able to tell me) was stationed in Lancashire, near to Blackpool, so we saw one another regularly. He was waiting to hear where his next posting after that would be. If we had lurched into the seemingly inevitable marriage by then, that might have some bearing on my future career move.

But for now, I had applied to and been accepted to work on the Stretford and Urmston Journal, a weekly newspaper in Greater Manchester. It was part of the Bolton Evening News group, owned then by Tillotsons Newspapers, who had a proud pedigree going back to 1867.

Fleet Street it was not. But it was a respectable enough group for which to work. My daily toil was to consist of anything and everything required to fill the pages of a local weekly newspaper, with an occasional piece for the Evening News itself, if something happened in our circulation area.

The office was a simple train journey from my parents' home which meant I could continue to live there until I knew where Destiny was set on taking me. It also meant I could spend most Saturdays up to my oxters in horse manure and saddle soap at the stables on Holiday Lane. I needed to have horse contact to get through my working week.

On Saturdays in the newspaper office, we worked a rota system where there was always one of us on duty, in exchange for which we had the Friday off. It meant working about one Saturday in four, which was not too bad. Especially as it was a quiet day and we could often slope off in the afternoon, before our normal finishing time of five-thirty.

'A gown of Guipure lace was chosen by bride ...'

'A honeymoon in the Seychelles followed the wedding on Saturday of ...'

'The bride's mother chose an ensemble in lavender blue at the wedding of ...'

No, that wasn't me planning mine. That was part of the daily grind of being a reporter on a local weekly paper. In those days, such papers had long and detailed reports of weddings and it was the job of some poor reporter to knock up something interesting from the bog-standard forms that were filled in at the front desk. These contained all the details of who was who, who wore what, what flowers were carried and so on. Bearing in mind that there might be a dozen or more to be done and they all had to have a different intro.

Muggins here got to do the lions' share, as the lads who had been doing them were more than happy to hand them on to the newest arrival. Sexism? No. Just traditional that the most junior staffer got the stuff the others didn't fancy. I also had endless sports reports dumped on me and I know nothing about sports. As long as one of the lads told me if the scoring was in points, tries, runs or goals, I could usually knock out something reasonable.

I was the only female in the office and I'd heard before I joined that Pissquick was not keen on females. I'd been appointed by the deputy editor-in-chief of the group and foisted on him, so I knew from the start I would have a hard job to win his approval. Funnily enough, it was a shared love of Irish folk music which won him over, rather than my journalistic skills.

Pissquick was managing editor of two weekly papers within the group, the one at Urmston, where I was to be based, and another on the other side of the Manchester Ship Canal at a place called Eccles. This gave him the perfect excuse to disappear out of either office for long periods of time, claiming to be going to the other office. We all knew perfectly well that he was, in fact, simply going to the nearest pub.

The drill was that we always covered for him. In exchange he could be surprisingly generous, always putting his hand in his pocket when we went to the pub with him at lunchtime, or on to the Conservative Club afterwards. The reason we went there was not political. It was simply that it stayed open after our local pub, The Victoria Arms, shut at lunchtime.

As the newest member of the team, I had the seat nearest to

the door, next to the telephones, which I was in charge of answering.

'Editorial,' I said brightly when I picked the phone up in response to its buzz one day.

'Can I speak to Maurice Brown, please?' the voice at the other end asked.

'I'm sorry, Mr Brown is out of the office at the moment. He's at our Eccles office.'

There was a long, audible sigh, then the voice explained patiently, 'This is the Eccles office.'

'Oh well, in that case, he's round at The Vic. He should be back just after stop-tap.'

Maurice Brown had, surprisingly, been a Commando back in the day, so when he discovered I was engaged to an Artillery officer, he insisted I should bring The Intended to meet him and there was a lot of military bonding over drinks in The Vic. Mind you, after about a gallon of mild and some gin, Pissquick was capable of bonding with anyone.

He loved dogs and once went home with a pup he'd bought from a man in a pub which he'd christened Sinatra because it had blue eyes. The trouble was that once he sobered up, he discovered that it didn't have blue eyes at all, that was just a trick of the light through beer goggles.

His military history was surprising because, these days, Pissquick could and often did sink about eight pints of mild in a session, and I dread to think how many packets of cigarettes he got through in a day. He was always asking one or another of us to pop out to the shop called 'Barmy Mick's' just down the road to buy him more smokes.

Depending on how much, or sometimes how little, alcohol he had consumed, his moods could change quickly. Unfortunately, he didn't sprout horns and a forked tail when he was in one of his blackest humours, so it was never clear what was in store for any of us when he came lurching back from The Vic at the end of lunchtime. He could be anything from morose and maudlin to downright menacing and obnoxious.

One of my doubtless many annoying habits is that I love to sing or hum a lot of the time and I particularly like folk music, Irish most of all. In the Journal office building, Pissquick's office was on the ground floor – ideal as sometimes the stairs were beyond him – and further along the passageway leading to it was a kitchen in a lean-to at the back of the building.

Everyone took turns in brewing up, so sexism was not rife there either. We dreaded it being Wilf, the sub-editor, who made tea so strong you could creosote a fence with it. Bob, the chief reporter, possibly brewed up fewer than anyone, but the other three reporters, Alistair, Steve and Trevor, all took their turn. This particular day it was my turn.

I was down in the kitchen waiting for the kettle to boil and was, as I often do, singing to myself as I waited. Pissquick's door burst open, he stuck his head out and growled in his deep voice, 'Les? Come in here.'

In those days I went by my birth-name, which I never liked. Tottie had not yet been invented as an alter ego.

Wondering what I'd done wrong, I headed for his office and went warily in.

'Was that you singing Four Green Fields?' he asked.

I was surprised he even knew the song. I hadn't learned, by this time, that his wife was from the Republic of Ireland and that he loved the Irish rebel songs as much as I did.

I nodded cautiously, still not sure where this conversation was going.

'Do you know Boolavogue?'

I resisted asking him, 'Is the Pope a catholic?' whilst wishing he hadn't picked that one. It was rather high for my contralto range, but I nodded again.

'Sing it,' he ordered.

So I did.

He seemed pleased.

It became a bit of a ritual.

Sometimes when he arrived back from his lunchtime sessions feeling a little more mellow than usual, the intercom buzzer on the phone next to my desk would sound. It always made a noise rather like a wet fart. Then Maurice's rather drunken voice would order, 'Les? Come down here and sing Boolavogue.'

The Intended also liked folk music, though not as passionately as I did. My brother and I would often take him out round the various folk clubs that we frequented in and around Stockport. My brother was always musical and one of the instruments he played was the tin whistle, a great favourite on Irish folk tracks.

Manchester and Stockport both have quite a history with the Irish and not always in a good way. Stockport even saw some anti-Irish riots in the 1850s. The situation in Ulster at this time was bad and getting progressively worse.

So it was probably not the best time, nor our best idea, for my brother and me, plus some of the Irish music fans from work, to decide to smuggle The Intended with us into an Irish Catholic social club in Manchester to see a live performance by The Dubliners.

One of the women from the advertising department of our paper was coming with us. She was bringing her husband, a Geordie photographer from one of the national dailies, who spent a lot of time in Ireland covering The Troubles. He'd met The Dubliners on a couple of occasions.

The evening was like nothing any of us had encountered before. It was wild. There was lots of Irish dancing, in between the singing sets, and the MC for the evening kept having to appeal for help in clearing all the empty beer bottles from the floor so the dancing could continue safely.

We all told The Intended that if he wanted any of us to get out of there alive, he should keep his trap shut for the entire evening, even for the singing. He had the sort of accent which screamed Sandhurst-trained British army officer.

We did all get out in one piece, slightly merry, very hoarse from singing, and more than a bit surprised to see half the Greater Manchester Police lined up in cars outside the club when we emerged and some ungodly hour past midnight.

Ever the journalist, I asked what was going on, hoping for a scoop. The police officers attending smiled indulgently and said it was just a normal turnout for closing time at that particular club.

Chapter Five
Everybody Out!

The Intended was staying in his posting near Blackpool for the time being. But at one point he was sent on a short secondment to Germany as a ski instructor in the Harz Mountains. Nice work if you can get it.

He suggested it might be fun if I went out to join him for a few days. It would, at least, give us a chance to spend a bit of proper time alone together. He planned on booking us into a small *pension*, where we would have our own small self-catering apartment with kitchenette. So we should, at least, not be disturbed by small nephews, vigilant parents, strict landladies, or anything else which had up to now been putting something of a damper on any attempts at a love-life.

I still wasn't convinced that love was the right word. I was fond of him, but I'd yet to experience any breathtaking moments of passion. I should, perhaps, also have paid more attention to a few Freudian indicators that perhaps this was not to be the true love of my life.

I was now sporting a very impressive Victorian-style five diamond gold engagement ring, duly made for me by The Intended's brother-in-law. It really was a lovely piece, a unique design, so it attracted a lot of attention.

It was strange, then, that I should manage to nearly lose it after I'd not had it for long. It was only pure luck that I got it back.

Back in those heady days, newspapers were edited to within an inch of their life before being inflicted on the paying public. I don't remember there being any free papers then. In our office we had the sub-editor, Wilf, who went over everything we wrote with a fine-tooth comb before sending it up to Bolton, where all the papers in the group were printed.

This was still in the time of hot metal presses, which seems positively Dickensian in these days of instant everything. The copy we wrote was set by linotype operators. A proof of what they set was then taken and this would be read by a formidable team known as Readers, whose job was to check for everything, not just typos, but ensuring clarification of meaning, too.

'Readers' would sometimes phone the satellite offices to check details with the reporter who had written a particular piece. I remember having a long conversation with one about my use of the expression 'stable name' for a horse. It's the opposite of 'kennel name' for a dog, which is its official name, whereas a 'stable name' is what the horse is known by on a daily basis.

I had to go to great lengths to convince the Reader that I did actually know about such things. I'd recently acquired my first dog, as I'd always wanted one. He was a big and handsome German Shepherd of impeccable pedigree, whose kennel name, registered with the Kennel Club, was Velindre Gorsefield Lobo. Far too much of a mouthful for everyday, so he was called Perro, which I quickly shortened to Pez for ease.

Once a week, on publication day, Pissquick, accompanied by Bob the chief reporter and another reporter chosen at random, often me, would travel up to Bolton to be there for six in the morning to do the next stage in checking all was as it should be, stone subbing, before the paper was printed.

The pages were assembled on long bench-like constructions known as a stone. Unions were strong in those days, especially in the print industry, and the rules were strictly upheld. One side of the stone was for the printers, usually from the NGA, the National Graphical Association, the other for the journalists, mostly NUJ, the National Union of Journalists.

The NGA back then were a tetchy lot, prone to walk out for the least thing. Strikes had been called over failure to respect the barrier between the two sides of the stone. I tended to stand with my hands in my pockets so I wouldn't be tempted to touch anything on 'their' side. But generally it was fairly harmonious.

If anything did happen to provoke an incident, one word – or rather two, the dreaded 'Everybody out!' - from an NGA shop steward could grind production to a halt in seconds.

Once a page had been put together, yet another proof was taken to be read by us, the stone subs. It was a fair bet that by this time not many errors had got through. There were inevitably a couple though, so the morning of publication day was always an anxious one in the office as the calls started to come in pointing out mistakes.

All that handling of proofs from the metal presses meant that by this stage our hands would be covered in printers' ink so we would need to wash them before going back to our own office. The bonus of our early start was that once we had taken the first copies, hot off the press, back to the office, we had the rest of the day off.

Soon after I started wearing the engagement ring, I followed the usual ritual of hand-washing. Afterwards I got almost all the way outside the building to the funky moped I was now riding to get to and from work, as there was no public transport which would get me to work that early, before I realised I had left my ring behind.

I flew back to the building and up the stairs, taking them several at a time, convinced I had seen the last of the ring and wondering how to explain my carelessness to The Intended. Mercifully, for once, the Bird of Paradise was smiling on me rather than crapping on me from a great height and it was still sitting there on the side of the washbasin where I'd left it.

But was that an omen? That it clearly meant so little to me that I could forget about it?

There was another possible pointer which I chose to ignore. My dog, Pez, was proving to be an excellent judge of character. He didn't suffer fools gladly and was particular who he took to. To my surprise, he had taken a liking to Pissquick, although he generally didn't like drunks. That confirmed my belief that deep inside that drink-raddled body was a fundamentally good man who had just lost his way.

Pez got on reasonably well with The Intended. But he was first and foremost my dog, and his self-appointed mission in life was to protect me against all comers. One day as The Intended and I were walking with Pez along the banks of the River Goyt in Stockport, he made the mistake of picking up a stick to throw for Pez but then pretending to attack me with it.

Dog 10, The Intended 0.

Pez leapt up and grabbed him none too gently but extremely firmly by the arm which was holding the stick.

Fortunately he was obedient and let go when I told him to, plus a heavy, padded ski jacket limited any damage to no more than some bruising. But he was clearly giving his opinion.

So it was going to be a good opportunity to get to know better the man I might be saddling myself with for the rest of my life, by going on this trip out to Germany to spend a bit of time alone with him.

Getting there was going to be something of an adventure. At this point I'd already flown a couple of times, on school exchange trips to France, and discovered that I hated it. Going by plane was out of the question, as far as I was concerned.

Transport out to the wilds of the Harz Mountains, more precisely to Braunlage, which was near to my destination, was not easy in those days. It was a ski resort but not one of the top fashionable ones bringing in thousands of tourists, so travel arrangements were limited.

I would need to take a ferry across the channel then a train to Hanover, where The Intended would meet me and drive us on to our destination.

My brother quite enjoyed travelling, despite always being sick, especially at sea. As he'd never visited Hanover before, he announced his intention to travel that far with me, then to make his own way back by whatever route took his fancy.

The Intended was at the station to meet us as planned. At least it was in the comfort of his Triumph Herald rather than a draughty Army Land Rover. Arrangements were so much harder to make back in the days before mobile phones. I'm not sure what I would have done if he hadn't been there. He and my brother got on reasonably well – another seal of approval. We had a quick drink together before my brother went off on whatever adventure he had planned in Hanover. I dreaded to think.

Meanwhile we drove back through snowy roads and dark forest tracks to the *pension* which was to be our 'home' for the few days I was staying there.

For the first time we were actually going to be sleeping together in the full sense of the phrase. Going to bed at the same time, making love, falling asleep then waking up together. A real try before you buy.

So this time did the earth move?

Certainly not enough to risk any avalanches in the snowy mountains outside.

Did angels sing?

Just a tentative note or two as if they were tuning up for the big performance which never quite happened.

It was okay. Nothing more.

The Intended was blissfully happy, wandering about with a soppy grin on his face most of the time.

I was left with that feeling you get sometimes from a book, film or play. It was all right, but there was some undefined ingredient missing to lift it above the mundane.

I like films. I relate to them. I went often with my father to press premières of newly-released films as he wrote reviews on them for his own and various other papers.

A controversial one of 1970 had been David Lean's Ryan's Daughter. The critics were divided on it. I loved it.

A tale of a publican's daughter in rural Ireland, a hopeless romantic, who sets her cap at the schoolmaster as the only likely catch. She's clearly expecting seismic earth movement.

There's a pivotal moment when she's talking to her parish priest about what marriage is all about. He, being celibate, admits he's not in a position to advise her on all aspects.

He sees her looking up at soaring sea birds and rightly interprets the look as her expecting things to change and her heart, at least, to take wing.

Those few nights in the little *pension* left me feeling like Sarah Miles in the film.

But hey, I'm an optimist. Perhaps things would get better as we got to know one another better.

Surely?

Chapter Six
Stop the World

Have you ever been in a vehicle when the brakes have failed? When you feel that gut-wrenching panic that you've lost all control? Or even on a bolting horse, with the same problem? I've ridden a few of those and it's not a nice feeling.

My impending wedding was starting to feel a bit like that. I kept trying to apply brakes which were just not responding. It had seemed like an abstract idea, something in the far future which would never happen. But now we were hurtling towards it at frightening speeds and no amount of determined pumping the brakes or take and give on the reins was having the slightest effect.

It was going to be quite an affair. There was a certain touch of irony about the date we'd chosen - 15th September, the anniversary of the Battle of Britain.

The marriage ceremony was going to take place at our local parish church, St Alban's, Offerton, where my father, often nicknamed Holy Joe by people who knew him, was sacristan and a licensed lay reader. He probably spent more time there than he did at home, certainly than with his children.

There would be a guard of honour, with some of The Intended's fellow officers in full dress uniform, holding up their ceremonial swords to form an arbour over our heads as we left the church.

My interests would be represented by one of my friends

from the riding school, who would ride to the ceremony on one of my favourite horses, Peter Piper. He was a black so with his feet painted in Stockholm tar and his mane plaited up with white roses, he looked a picture.

We were to be married by no fewer than three priests. So the knot would be well and truly tied. My father had spent his war years, in the Royal Air Force, in Rhodesia, as it was then. As a journalist with good shorthand (Pitman) and typing skills, he was on the court martial circuit taking and transcribing notes. He also edited the RAF in Africa newsletter, AFRAF. He didn't see active service but he did manage to be injured and eventually invalided out. Not by enemy action but by being stung on the foot by a scorpion.

Whilst visiting Johannesburg he had met priests there from an Anglican religious order, the Community of the Resurrection, who were based in Mirfield, West Yorkshire. He'd become great friends with a young African priest, Fr Leo Rakale.

Fr Leo had made the long journey from Africa to the UK to officiate at my parents' wedding, just after the war. He'd managed to get as far as Liverpool but post-war fuel rationing had meant he could get no further. So my father had invited him to come and officiate at my wedding.

He was also my brother's godfather, so it would be an opportunity for him to see something of his godson, as visits from Africa were few and far between.

Fr Leo was, in his quiet way, something of a celebrity. He was the inspiration behind the character of Msimangu in Alan Paton's novel about Africa, *Cry, the Beloved Country,* who was played in the film of the book by Sidney Poitier.

Father continued his contact with the brethren of the Community throughout his life. Growing up, my brother and I were often left being babysat by various strange young celibate priests and missionaries, and there was a procession of visiting priests and even the odd bishop or two to our house. There was some degree of scandal later on involving one of the bishops following his public admission to a fondness for fondling young boys' bottoms. I often wonder if anything like ever that went on under our roof.

Another priest my father had known for years, also connected to the Community, Fr Harold, would be officiating at my marriage. He was a frequent visitor to our house. I have memories of him being taxed with escorting me to the riding stables when I was small and neither parent was available to take me.

For the sake of diplomacy, our own parish priest was also to take a small part in the ceremony, so one way or another, we were going to be well and truly married.

The reception was to be held at a smart Cheshire country hotel, Mottram Hall. An elegant 18th century Georgian country house, set in two hundred and seventy acres, with a magnificent lake, it would be ideal for those wedding photos. My father's staff photographer was to be behind the lens. He had all sorts of ideas, wanting to come round to the house to photograph me getting ready, putting on my make-up, all that palaver.

I've never been a typically girly girl. Not into hair and make-up, nor clothes, particularly. I'd indulged Auntie Ethel by letting her have free rein on my dress, going for fittings and standing patiently while she stuck pins here and there as she made tweaks. Never in me, she was far too professional for that.

I'd had to remove Pez, my dog, and put him outside the first time she started attacking me with the pins. He didn't approve of that at all and made his feelings clear with ominous, rumbling growls in the way of threats.

As far as any other beautification went, I would twist my hair up and plonk a comb and a veil there to keep it in place and slap on a bit of make-up. But no more than that. Certainly nothing worth taking photos of.

Military friends of The Intended had been horrified to discover that instead of jetting off somewhere exotic – A honeymoon in the Seychelles followed the wedding of – we were instead going to stay in a small B&B in the Scottish Highlands, near to Oban, for a fortnight. And my dog Pez was coming with us.

Lying about on sandy beaches would be the stuff of my worst nightmares, especially if they involved a long plane journey to get there. I liked the wide open spaces, hills and mountains, walking, communing with nature, watching wild birds, especially big raptors. Luckily The Intended – I suppose I would soon have to get used to the dreaded 'My Husband and I' - was not averse to that sort of thing.

It would be a long old drive up to Oban after the reception so we had arranged to break the journey by staying a night at a motel near to Bolton. My parents had eaten and stayed there once on some official function or another and declared it quite acceptable.

At some point during our engagement, I'd decided to swear off the demon drink completely. Working in the office with Pissquick was becoming perilous as drinking was so much a part of the culture. Lunchtimes were often spent in The Vic and when we did all finally troop back to work, slightly the worse for wear, our inebriated editor would frequently send someone out to get more drink to see us through the afternoon.

Apart from what it was doing to my liver, it had been harmless enough when I had been commuting on the train. But once I'd got the moped, I had to knock it on the head. The drink-driving laws had come into effect in the mid-60s and I couldn't afford to lose my licence. I have no idea how Pissquick managed to keep his. I can only assume he was known to the police and they opted to turn a blind eye for some reason. Perhaps it was to do with funny handshakes. Masonic membership was as common in journalism as in the police force, although my father avoided it with a passion.

I'd already had one accident on the moped. Not my fault, and nothing to do with alcohol. A woman emerging from a side street had simply not seen me until the last minute, then had slammed on her brakes right in front of me. It was undeniably her fault and I successfully sued her, allowing me to buy a small minivan to replace the crumpled moped.

Turning teetotal had its drawbacks. I saw things as they were, rather than through a euphoric, alcoholic haze. I definitely saw that The Intended was more of a clown than I'd thought previously. But somehow the runaway train effect of the wedding was beyond stopping by now. I would just have to make the best of things – or take up drinking again. If you can't beat them, join them.

It took quite a bit of forward planning to sort out getting Pez and the Triumph Herald to the hotel so we could make our departure from there. There was one big advantage of having seven stone of ferocious guard-dog in our get-away vehicle. No one could get near it to do any of the usual nonsense of covering it in shaving foam, filling our luggage up with confetti or tying tin cans and old boots to the back bumper.

As I was the sober one, I would be driving the first leg to where we would be spending our wedding night. The following day, on our onward journey, we could share the driving, making frequent stops to walk Pez and see something of the scenery through which we were passing.

I believe it's traditional for the bride's mother (certainly in those days) to have a word with her daughter about the wedding night. I didn't expect any such conversation with my mother. Her relationship with my father was so bizarre I had a strong suspicion she'd only had sex twice in her life – my brother, and me. My brother, on the other hand, was convinced she had had some mad passionate liaison with our father's brother and that he was the result of that. But this was a theory he espoused in later life when the drink had done a lot of damage to his thought processes, so I tended to discount it.

In fact I'll draw a veil over the whole of the wedding night. A combination of a rather drunken bridegroom and possibly the noisiest venue we could have chosen, resulting in Pez giving woofs of disapproval throughout the night, made it a less than memorable occasion.

The honeymoon itself was nice enough. The days, at least. We walked a lot, saw raptors, went on a boat trip and saw seals. Lots of scenery and wildlife. We discovered a folk club and went there a few times.

Our landlady was kindness itself. She'd stressed that she did B&B only with 'nothing' in the evenings, except perhaps a cup of tea. Mrs Clark's 'nothings' became a source of amusement to us. The first evening, we'd gone out and eaten fish and chips on the seafront then arrived back at the B&B to be confronted with cake and scones and more cake, Scotch pancakes and Selkirk bannocks. Plus enough tea to float a battleship.

After the first evening we gave up on evening meals altogether and just braced ourselves for the 'nothings'. Pez obligingly helped us out on more than one occasion as Mrs Clark was mortified if we didn't eat everything in sight.

And then there were the night-times, in our cosy double bed. Still the earth didn't move and the angels didn't sing. But it was all right. We seemed happy enough. We got back from our honeymoon to find my mother had spent the time completely redecorating my old bedroom and replacing my single bed with a double so we could sleep there together, as man and wife.

Because we were now man and wife. Well and truly shackled. Bound by the hand of god and by three priests.

'What therefore God hath joined together, let not man put asunder.'

Chapter Seven
Husband's Last Three

The honeymoon was over, literally, and life was going back to how it was before. Except I was now sporting a second ring on the third finger of my left hand and calling myself Mrs G.

I didn't like my new surname much and you don't really need to know it for the purposes of the book, so let's stick with Mrs G. for now. Except, as I was soon to discover, when you married into the Army back then, you lost all personal identity and became known, all too often, as simply 'wife of'. If I'd read that in the small print, I would have tried much harder to put the brakes on before it had got this far.

The Other Half had now got his next posting. He was going to be playing Thunderbirds on Salisbury Plain. I should perhaps explain. The new regiment to which he was posted was an air defence one, intended to protect British skies against attack from all comers. And one of the weapons in their arsenal at the time was the Thunderbird missile.

As well as his new posting, he had also acquired a third pip, making him a Captain. There were so many things about his role that I didn't know – and I confess to not being all that interested in – but he was going to be doing something responsible in a unit of a regiment, called a Battery.

Batteries often held specific battle honours for having done something notable in some historical campaign. His was known as The Broken Wheel Battery after some calamity had befallen it in the Battle of Tel-el-Kebir in the Egyptian War of 1882.

It was apparently something significant because when Pez, the dog, and I, moved down to join him on Salisbury Plain, he got my mother and my auntie to make a special coat for Pez in the battery colours of maroon and gold so he could wear it and parade with the Battery as a sort of mascot. The Other Half also got his jeweller brother-in-law to make gold brooches in the shape of a wheel with a piece broken out of it. Not the most attractive look, but apparently one had to support the Battery at all costs.

I still had a good few months to run on my indentures with the newspaper. In those days, an apprenticeship was a pretty serious affair. You literally sold your soul to your new masters until you had worked your time, and you were supposed to inform them of each and every change in your circumstances.

As a matter of form, I'd notified Pissquick of my nuptials and had even invited him to the wedding. He didn't attend, but he did buy us a generous gift.

The Other Half was pining for me – sweet! We saw one another most weekends. Either he would drive up to see me or Pez and I would drive down there. But he wanted me to move down there to live, with promises of being able to have a nice house on The Patch, which is a universal name given to military housing everywhere. In our case it would be The Officers' Patch in Bulford Camp.

I explained that it wasn't entirely up to me. I could ask the Editor-in-chief of the group if I could be released early from my indentures, but explained that if he said no, I would just have to work my ticket and join him when that was done.

I never expected my Editor-in-chief to agree. I was rather counting on him not doing so. According to Pissquick, he went seven shades of ballistic when he got my letter. But when he had simmered down, he agreed that I could finish at the end of the year, six months before my due time.

I never liked to use any influence of my father to get what I wanted within journalism. But it may have been no coincidence that my father and my Editor-in-chief knew one another through the Guild of British Newspapers, and through the National Council for the Training of Journalists.

Fate was, it seemed, conspiring against me. I had been hoping it would obligingly throw obstacles in my way to delay the seemingly inevitable. Instead, it was opening doors for me.

To make a show, more than anything, I'd been enquiring about local newspaper jobs near to Bulford Camp, as I had no intentions of becoming a lady of leisure. I'd found that there was an immediate vacancy for a general reporter on a local paper, or rather two papers, since they were both produced from the same office. The Salisbury Times and Journal were part of the Berrows group, the oldest local newspaper group in Britain.

So, some six months earlier than I had intended, I loaded myself and Pez up, together with the most treasured of my possessions, into my minivan and headed off down the motorway to start a new phase of my life as 'wife of'.

The trip down was not without adventure. It was cold, to say the least, well below freezing. The heater in the little minivan was about as effective as blowing on your hands when you had frostbite. I was wearing the big hippy Afghan coat I'd bought for myself from the sales in Bolton early one morning, actually queuing up on the doorstep because I'd always wanted one.

My mother was horrified and refused to have it in the house. I had to take it off on arrival and leave it either in Barney, my van (I name absolutely everything) or hanging up in the garage. It did smell rather rank, but I loved it. And I was certainly glad of its hairy warmth on that chilly drive.

As I trundled my way south, I was surprised to find myself being pulled over by the police. The minivan was too slow to be exceeding any speed limits. All the lights were working perfectly well. I was driving safely and sensibly, and I was certainly alcohol-free since I no longer drank at all.

A police officer came to the driver's door and motioned to me to wind the window down. Only in those old vans they didn't wind, they slid to the side. And because the temperature inside was barely higher than that outside, it was frozen shut.

Pez, by this stage, was decidedly not amused to see a strange man trying to gain entry into his mistress's vehicle and was showing his disapproval by loud, ferocious barking. He was also trying to hurl himself over my shoulder and out of the window to seize the offender warmly by the throat.

I was worried that if I shouldered the door to open it, so I could at least talk to the officer, Pez would see his opportunity and be out of the gap in an instant with murder most foul on his mind. Not a good idea, on a busy motorway hard shoulder, when dealing with a policeman.

Luckily, the policeman, who had been shining his torch into the van and could by now see that there was only me and some wolf-like murderous creature in the back, was smiling at me. He explained that they were randomly stopping vans in connection with serious sexual assaults. But as he could see that I was not a rapist, there was no need to detain me.

He was, he said, supposed to be warning lone female drivers about the potential dangers. Having seen my passenger, he said he didn't think I was in any danger and wished me a safe journey.

The good thing about married quarters in those days, especially for officers, was that they came fully equipped and ready to move into without the need of any additional possessions. The furniture was not always in brilliant taste, but it was functional.

We had been allocated a reasonable-sized detached three-bedroom house at the end of a cul-de-sac. It was set back, at right angles to the neighbouring houses, and with a decent bit of garden running round all four sides, it felt nicely secluded.

It had a garage and next to the garden was what I, being from 'oop north', would call a ginnel, a passageway, a footpath, between the houses which led to an open green space, bisected by a road. It meant I didn't have far to go to exercise my dog.

The big disadvantage of this type of house, as I quickly discovered, was that the windows were not double-glazed and the metal frames were draughty. It took quite a bit of keeping warm.

The other thing I soon found out was that living on The Patch was like living in a goldfish bowl. Everyone knew everybody else's business, whether they wanted to or not.

Our immediate neighbours, a cavalry officer, his wife, their small child and a Weimeraner dog, were volatile, to say the least. The first time, not long after I'd moved in there, that a screaming row broke out, I wasn't sure what the form was. Did one just turn a polite blind eye and hope all would soon calm down, or summon urgent assistance?

One time in the middle of one such argument, when I saw the wife storming from the garage to the main house brandishing a large pair of garden shears and screaming, 'Right, that's it, you've gone too far this time', I did wonder whether it would be appropriate to call the Military Police.

We found out later on the grapevine, as absolutely nothing was a secret on The Patch, that the shears were meant for his clothes, not him. The row had started because he was going away on exercise and she had not ironed his shirts as requested.

She'd apparently dealt with his disapproval by taking the shears to everything then had finished up by pouring custard into his kitbag.

Never a dull moment in the life of a new Army wife.

My next rude awakening was to the total loss of my identity as a person in my own right. I was fortunate to enjoy good health but The Other Half said I should go and register myself at the Family Medical Centre as soon as possible, just in case.

I went to the reception area where a one-striper, not in the Artillery regiment so presumably a Lance Corporal, immediately got out his forms when I began to speak, without so much as giving me a glance.

I started by giving my name, which seemed like a good beginning but with a barely concealed sigh, he asked, 'Wife of?'

Surprised, I nevertheless gave him The Other Half's name, rank and regiment, which was about all I knew about him.

Another sigh, with more than a hint of impatience this time.

'Husband's last three?'

He had me there, completely. I had no idea what last three might be of interest to a medical centre. Always cursed with something of a lavatorial sense of humour, I was fighting down giggles as all I could come up with at the time was bowel movements.

I was rapidly dismissed and ordered to come back when I knew the last three digits of my husband's service number, whatever that was.

So now I was to be known not only as 'wife of' but as 'husband's last three'

I was reminded of the cult 60s TV series, The Prisoner.

I felt like standing there shouting, 'I am not a number. I am a free woman!'

I meekly went back to The Patch to find out my husband's last three.

Chapter Eight
Stranger than Fiction

When you write fiction, especially crime as I do now, you will very quickly get pulled up by critical readers for putting too much reliance on coincidence as a device. But they clearly forget that real life is often far stranger than fiction. Only yesterday I heard the tale of someone whose ex had married a person called Ann Marie when the names of the children they had had together were Ann and Marie.

On my first day at my new newspaper office, I presented myself at the front desk as instructed and they called upstairs on the intercom for someone to come down from the editorial office to escort me to my new desk. Presumably in case I got lost on the way.

Who should come clumping down the stairs and then collapse in giggles at the sight of me but someone with whom I had been on the course at Preston just a few months previously. Louise, as she was called, had gone to a job on a paper in Worcester, so I was not expecting to see her again. It turned out that she was also now courting an Army officer and had followed him to Salisbury Plain. As the Salisbury paper was in the same group as the Worcester one, it had been simple enough for her to make the transfer.

Once upstairs, I met the rest of the team, including a reporter called Fiona who had done her pre-entry training at Sheffield and had therefore had the dubious honour of having been lectured by my father on occasion.

Coincidences? Real life is full of them.

The new office was going to be a complete change from the days of Pissquick and the Urmston Journal. No long boozy lunches, certainly no drinking in the office. There was at least one strict Methodist on the management team to discourage any such goings on.

We had an editor who tended to stay in his office rather more than Pissquick had done. We certainly weren't on familiar drinking terms with him. There were several local editions of the same paper so we had an office full of sub-editors, plus a sports editor and a separate sports reporter. There was even a woman's page, with its own editor who came in a couple of days a week and hot-desked with a semi-retired journalist who wrote various features. He was the uncle of the chief reporter.

Said chief reporter was a strange person indeed.

Like most newspaper offices in those days, there was a cleaner who came in when the office was empty to give it a good clean and a polish. Yet every morning, without fail, the chief reporter would come in, shove her typewriter to the far side of the desk, pull out a tin of Pledge and a duster and polish it to within an inch of its life. With my sense of humour, I was sorely tempted to one day replace the polish spray with one with the same coloured cap but full of paint. I did manage to restrain myself, though.

She had a strange Tourette-like habit of blurting out bizarre words, sayings and even animal noises at odd and often somewhat inappropriate moments.

Salisbury is a cathedral city and the life in and around the Cathedral was often a source of news and features to the local paper.

I can remember being on the phone to the Dean one time and having to explain that no, there wasn't a small, hysterically barking dog in the office. It was just our chief reporter, having one of her funny turns.

We had a deputy chief reporter who was by day not a bad journalist and by night a drummer of some repute. Apparently he had played with Thin Lizzy. Add into the mix a handful of other reporters, John, Paul, Steven and Mark. They sound like apostles, listed like that. Each had their own speciality, be it general news, features writing, sports or whatever.

I was going to be doing a lot of court and coroner's court reporting in my new job. I hadn't done court reporting on the previous paper as they had a regular freelancer for that, but I had done inquests. Rather a lot of them. And I have to confess to having a certain morbid fascination for them. The one certainty in life is that one day, sooner or later, we are all going to die. It's just a question of when and how.

Back to my earlier point about coincidence. I would also cite my inquest experience which leads me to say to people, don't tell me such and such a thing would never happen because I will tell you the inquest I covered when it did.

Inquests were usually held at the local hospital and despite the inherent sadness of any death, they could sometimes result in moments of humour. Great self-control was often needed in the press bench to maintain a straight face and the proper amount of decorum when listening to evidence which tickled our collective funny bones. It only needed one reporter to lose it, even for just a moment, for the whole press pack of us to be crying with stifled tears of laughter. Not a good look in front of grieving relatives.

Courts, too, provided us with more than our fair share of chuckles, with some of the excuses for crimes the defendants came up with. Like the young man on a string of motoring offences who, when challenged about defective windscreen wipers, simply smiled and said he only took his car out when the sun was shining. Even some of the magistrates were seen to lower their heads to hide their smiles at that especially delivered as it was in a West Indian drawl by a dreadlocked Rasta.

As well as me from the local weekly paper, there would often be court reporters from the regional evening and daily papers at the hearings. One of them, a man called Don, was quite a liability to sit next to in court.

Magistrates in Britain are not required to have any form of legal training or qualification. They receive basic training for their role and are advised on matters of law by the clerk of the court, who is qualified. The clerk sometimes has to scramble to get them back on track when they try to pass a stronger sentence than they are allowed to.

Don, on the other hand, had a very respectable law degree and held the magistrates in open total contempt. Unfortunately, he had a voice which carried and in quieter moments, he would keep up a scathing monologue, pouring scorn on the unfortunate Justices of the Peace sitting up on the bench, who could doubtless hear every word he said. And he couldn't care less if they did.

'Look at him! Just look at him,' he would sneer. 'He's a brush salesman. A bloody brush salesman. What's he doing sitting up there in judgement on anyone?'

One chairman of the bench, a local landowner, had a most unusual name. I wasn't involved in stone subbing on this paper and I dread to think what happened to whoever was with the resulting typo. We were never sure whether it was accident or malice on the part of a linotype operator and I'm not sure if I'll get into terrible trouble for repeating this anecdote. I'll do my best to report it slightly censored.

The surname in question was Rhind-Tutt. Well known, well respected in the area. Nothing at all to do with parts of a rhinoceros's anatomy. Not, I repeat, not, Rhino-Tw*t, which is what appeared in the paper.

There were also some awkward moments in court, when I encountered people I knew from the same military circles as

The Other Half.

The Royal Artillery had its own hunt. A fox hunt back in the day, before the hunting of animals ban. And because I despise hypocrisy, I will admit to having hunted with them on occasion. I was a different person back then. It could have been embarrassing when the Master of the hunt appeared in court to answer a charge of riding a motor cycle without a helmet. Apparently he had his riding hat on instead. Luckily there were several courtrooms within the building and I was in another one, reporting on more serious things than minor traffic offences. I still had to write up his appearance for the paper, though.

By now I knew a lot of people from The Other Half's Regiment, and from the Battery in particular. There was a bit of a ground-swallowing moment when I was sent to report on Juvenile Court one day. It's not called that now, it's Young Offenders, which somehow makes it all seem less serious. Of course these days some youngsters have shown themselves capable of committing crimes every bit as heinous as any adult.

The general public are not allowed into such courts. The Press are, but the regulations on what they can report are very strict. I tried to make myself look inconspicuous when the door opened and in walked another Bomb, a Bombardier from The Other Half's Battery. But it was a small room, an intimate setting, and it was impossible for him to fail to see me sitting there, desperately trying to look as if I wasn't taking notes of everything which was said.

His small son, only just old enough to be in a court of law, was being charged with several burglaries. That was bad enough, but he also asked for a staggering number of similar offences to be taken into consideration.

At least the Bombardier left the court immediately after the hearing and didn't hang around to make any attempt to ask me not to report it. It was always difficult when someone did that, especially after an inquest. It always sounded trite to trot out the 'I'm just doing my job' line, but I was and it was not up to me what was or was not published in the paper.

I'd had a gruelling time once after an inquest into a Sudden Infant Death when the distraught parents had besieged me, begging me not to publish it in the paper.

To make matters worse on that day in Juvenile Court, I'd already had an embarrassing encounter with the same Bombardier at one of the dreaded social occasions I had to attend with The Other Half and usually hated every minute of.

A classless society the Army certainly was not during the 1970s. For social functions, the officers had their own Mess where anyone not commissioned as an officer was not allowed to set foot – unless it was to wait on at table. Sergeants had their own Mess where occasionally officers were invited for special occasions but anyone lower down the rankings was kept out. Then there was the NCOs' Mess, for non-commissioned officers, the Corporals and Lance Corporals, or Bombardiers and Lance Bombardiers, depending on the Regiment.

We'd been invited to some sort of a function in the NCOs' Mess. I can't remember what the occasion was. Or rather, the excuse, as I discovered that in the Army, any day could be turned into a reason to party. So we'd have Christmas parties, New Years' parties, Twelfth Night parties. Not to mention all the patron saints days for the various regiments of England, Scotland, Wales and Northern Ireland – St George, St Andrew, St David, St Patrick, not forgetting, St Barbara, who is patron saint of artillery. Literally any excuse.

This particular evening was going to include <shudder> party games. I absolutely loathe and detest any such thing. I'm not too bad at charades, if pressed, and am determined, just once before I die, to try karaoke because I like singing. But party games are not my thing at all.

I've no idea what it was called but the game in question involved women in one circle, men in the other, inner, one.

Music was played, we had to move round, rather like in musical chairs. When the music stopped, we had to jump on the back of the nearest man. The female slowest to react was out of the game.

It wasn't the Officers' Mess so I wasn't in a long dress. In fact it was quite a short one. The nearest man to me was The Other Half's Bombardier. I'm used to vaulting onto horses, so jumping on his back was not difficult of itself. But in doing so, the dress rode right up my legs so the only way Bomb could hold onto me as required was with his hands on the top of my naked thighs.

I'm not sure which one of us was the more excruciatingly embarrassed.

The next time there was a function in the NCOs' Mess, I scheduled a migraine.

Chapter Nine
Time for a Change

The redeeming feature, for me, of life as an officer's wife on Salisbury Plain, was the Royal Artillery Saddle Club. It became my new place of refuge, my surrogate Holiday Lane.

People with their own horses could keep them there at livery. But the stable also provided horses for hire for non horse owners who might want a day's outing with the RA Hunt. The horses belonging to the hunt servants, the Whippers-in, Field Master and other staff, were also kept there.

The hunt met twice a week so horses hunting with them needed to be maintained at a suitable level of fitness. This meant them being exercised four times a week, hunted twice a week, then enjoying one day of rest, usually a Sunday.

Once you'd shown that you could ride well enough and could be trusted, other halves of military personnel were allowed to take the hunters out for exercise on Salisbury Plain, at no charge. The Plain is an elevated chalk upland, giving some three hundred square miles of wonderful riding country. Perfect for blowing away the cobwebs of stuffy Army life.

I didn't mind what I rode, as long as I could get out there, on my own, and have fun. I was happy to take out anything which needed the work. I didn't even mind the supposed old plodders as I've always had what's known as an electric seat. Just by sitting on it, I can usually rev up a rocking horse into an exciting ride.

So I rode everything I was offered. The Steady Eddies, like Tony and Ballyclare. The livelier but safe so-called 'ladies' rides' like the wonderful Haymarket, and pretty, grey Gub Gub, named after Dr Dolittle's friend the pig. Right up to the First Whip's horse, the big dark brute Polaris, and the Second Whip's tank of a mount, Tango, seemingly not fitted with brakes of any description, although mercifully the steering usually worked.

Sometimes I would hack horses to wherever the hunt was meeting for the person who was going to be hunting them for the day. Anything for a free ride!

I'd always wanted a horse of my own when growing up. My parents had insisted there wasn't the money for it. Since moving to Bulford, I'd acquired my first pony. A school-friend had a Welsh Mountain Pony mare of reasonable breeding so had offered me the first-born foal at a sensible price. I'd agreed and we'd taken delivery of a bright bay almost-yearling colt, who was now at livery at the Saddle Club, still looking tiny in the smallest available stable.

His registered name was Winsome Welshman, Taffy, to his friends. But we soon discovered he had such an evil disposition he was later to be known as Damien the Antichrist, after the character in The Omen books and films.

Hunters are traditionally not worked at all through much of the summer. They are roughed off and turned away once the hunting season is over. They do little more than gorge on grass until they are brought back up again to be got fit for the start of the new season. For the RA Saddle Club horses, this meant being let loose in a huge area of Salisbury Plain inside an electric ring fence.

The trouble is that Taffy, like most ponies, especially Welshies, was as sharp as a barrel-load of monkeys. He knew that touching the fence got him an electric shock. He also knew that the pain was fleeting and if he put up with it, the reward was total freedom, with the whole Plain as his personal playground.

Of course, once he'd shoulder-charged and broken the wire, there was a gap through which the bigger hunters could also fit, to join him on his adventures.

The Other Half was mortified one time when a major NATO exercise had to be halted because Taffy and his chums were busy playing 'Catch me if you can' on the impact area. The incident was not well received in military circles, although I saw the funny side of it.

Sometimes not all the horses were brought up at the end of summer. Any of them who were convalescing or those who were not in work for any reason, might enjoy a longer taste of leisure whilst their stable-mates were back under saddle.

One day the hunt was meeting at the hound kennels, a short hack away from the stables, across the Plain. So rather than bother getting the lorries out, the Hunt staff were riding across. I was riding something to deliver to one of the kennels staff.

The Master was at the front and his horse suddenly started to get a bit lively having heard a sudden noise behind us. We all looked round to see what had upset it. There, trotting along behind like a pet dog, was Taffy. My pony. The Master was not amused, asking if anyone knew who the little beast belonged to.

Like Judas Iscariot, I denied him, whilst surreptitiously trying to poke him with my hunting whip, hoping that would deter him enough for him to turn tail and trot off back home.

'I'm not sure, Master,' I said evasively, whilst muttering under my breath, 'bugger off, Taffy, go back home, you little perisher.'

Poke, poke, poke.

It was not the last of Taffy's escapades. The Other Half and I had to spend an embarrassing evening one time trying to catch him while he went skipping round a nearby graveyard, grabbing mouthfuls of flowers from the graves. I don't think anyone at the Saddle Club was sorry to see him go when we eventually moved him to a new home.

Life was jogging along on The Patch. I was finding it hard to form any kind of bond with other Army wives. We seemed to have little in common. They were, in the main, obsessed with looking after their husbands and producing children. The fact that I not only went out to work, unlike the majority of the others, but was clearly not planning on producing the required heir, never mind the spare, was openly frowned upon.

I had to bite my tongue nearly in half when we were invited round to the house of an officer The Other Half had met so I could meet his wife. They seemed to have a football team's worth of small ankle-biters already. Perhaps the idea was to encourage me into feeling broody. It had quite the opposite effect.

As we were getting ready to leave, the wife was looking reproachfully at my youthful and definitely not matronly figure. I've always had a somewhat boyish shape. In those days I still had the coveted 22-inch waist, with snake-hips and no boobs to speak of.

In a tone like a school mistress, she informed me, 'The next time I see you, I shall expect you to have at least a bump, if not a baby.'

A comment like that must be one of the most effective forms of birth control there is. It quite put me off the idea of sex.

It was about this time that the Bryan Forbes film, The Stepford Wives, came out. One of the perks of working on the local paper was that the office had a free pass for the local cinema in return for reviews of any films being shown there.

By this time, I'd taken in a lodger. Ann, a girl I'd known through the Holiday Lane stables at home in Stockport, was having a bit of a rough time at home. Her parents had mapped out for her a future career in teaching. Unfortunately, it was not what she wanted. I'd offered her somewhere to stay for a bit while things settled down.

At the same time, I'd taken a horse on loan. A big chestnut beast, Polish bred, called Tzigan, which is a word for gypsy, although not in Polish. Ann could ride well enough and jumped at the chance to exercise Tig-pig for me, as he became known, when I was working and the evenings were too dark for me to ride him out as there was no indoor school at the Saddle Club.

In addition I was quite glad of the company. If I had discovered that I had little in common with The Wives on The Patch, I was also finding out that I had less in common with The Other Half than I'd realised. We went places together, did things as a couple, but there was still that nagging feeling that there was something missing.

I took Ann with me to the cinema to see The Stepford Wives, as The Other Half was doing something soldierly in the Mess, which gave me a good excuse. And suddenly, it all made sense. I now knew why the Army Wives I was meeting were like they were!

Seriously, you need to see the film if you've not already done so. I was playing the Katharine Ross role and I hadn't realised it.

It made me determined to find the escape tunnel from life on The Patch, even if I had to dig it for myself. With my bare hands. Perhaps if we had a place to call our own and live a normal, non-military life, outside working hours, things might be better between me and The Other Half.

They weren't bad. Don't get me wrong. We muddled along. But the more time I spent with him, the more his playing the clown grated on my nerves. I didn't think it could be all that good for his career prospects, either. Not that that bothered me. But constantly blurting out stupid remarks and laughing at his own jokes didn't inspire a lot of confidence in his leadership skills.

We started looking about for a house to buy. We found quite a nice old rustic cottage in a village not far away, with what seemed like a reasonable sized garden. It was within our budget. I started to get excited. Except when we looked again, some boundary pegs had been put in to mark out what land was included in the sale – much less than we had been led to believe. Not enough to make it of interest to us.

Time for the famous Plan B. I always have a Plan B, to everything. I can't function without one.

Much to everyone's surprise, given his long history of travel sickness and particularly of seasickness, my brother had joined the Royal Fleet Auxiliary. He'd appeared at my wedding sporting his First Officer's uniform and had gone to sea on board the RFA Olwen, a fast-fleet tanker. One of his first tours of duty was the Second Cod War between the United Kingdom and Iceland.

After that the ship had been to Canada, which was where he'd met, and fallen madly in love with, a nurse called Deborah. They were planning their wedding and where they were going to live. Debs, as she preferred to be called, was at the time a theatre sister at a London hospital, but was quite happy to move.

She and I got on well, especially after we discovered a mutual love of horses and other animals. Debs was adamant that wherever they bought a house, she wanted to be able to keep at least one horse. She loved riding and hunting.

House-hunting these days is so easy, thanks to the internet. Back then it was less so. My brother had been doing his homework and had discovered that one of the best places at the time for getting value for money on property with land was West Wales.

He and Debs had already started looking. My brother had seen a place he had thought would be ideal. A large detached farmhouse with a barn and other outbuildings, plus ten acres of land with the option to buy another ten. It sounded amazing, especially as it was slightly less than the small semi-detached cottage we'd been looking at in Wiltshire.

Apparently the track up to the house was overgrown and Debs had pronounced it too dull and gloomy for her taste. But my brother was convinced it was a good bargain so wondered if it might be of any interest to us.

We hadn't thought of anywhere so far away from Salisbury Plain. But it made a lot of sense, and not just financially.

If we went back to living apart and seeing one another just at the weekends, perhaps it might kindle a spark and liven up our marriage. It was certainly worth a weekend away to take a look.

Chapter Ten
I Bought a Mountain

One of the differences between The Other Half and me was that I've always loved camping. I'm a big kid at heart. Any excuse to sleep in a tent. He didn't like it. To be fair to him, that's because he had to do a lot of it when he went away on exercise. So for his holidays, he preferred something with a few more home comforts.

Before we were married, we'd gone away together and I'd let him choose the destination and the accommodation. He'd opted for Cornwall and had booked us into a hotel at a place called Praa Sands, pronounced locally as Pray Sands. His family loved Cornwall. His parents went every year to a rented cottage in Boscastle. I'd never been further west than Devon so was happy to try it.

I found it strangely claustrophobic. All those narrow lanes with high banks hemming them in. I'm not a lover of the sea, so I preferred to venture inland. But I didn't find the wide-open spaces and mountain scenery which I liked best.

Holidays highlighted another difference in the backgrounds of The Other Half and me. His family did the normal things of going on holiday together. We didn't. I can remember very few proper family holidays in my childhood. We went to Lytham St Annes once, and to visit the family in Luxembourg. The rest of the time it was always to stay with my mother's family in St Helens. I realised much later in life that my brother had a lot of problems which caused awkward moments staying in holiday accommodation but were just about manageable with family.

Father was always pleading poverty although he can't have been all that badly off as a newspaper editor with a company car. Again, with the benefit of hindsight, I did wonder where his money went. Perhaps to the children of the missions in Africa, in which case, I don't begrudge them that. Even if it stopped me having a pony.

We did have some nice trips occasionally, though. Life-changing, in a way, for me, at least. Through the Editors' Guild, my father met a colourful character from North Wales who owned a number of local papers in the days when many were still privately owned. He had a holiday cottage near Bala, in North Wales, which he lent us on a couple of occasions for a family holiday.

It was a remote place, accessible by such a rough mountain track that an old Ford shooting brake was provided for visitors to get up and down, safely leaving their own vehicle parked at the bottom. I loved every minute spent there. The isolation. The total darkness, with no light pollution. The smell of wood-smoke on damp evening air. It was my idea of heaven.

Not long after our first visit I read Thomas Firbank's book '*I bought a mountain*' and fell even more in love with the whole idea of remote Welsh farmhouses. You can see where this is going, can't you? The prospect of going to visit an old Welsh farmhouse that might possibly become ours was so exciting for me.

The property was standing empty. We'd phoned to arrange to meet the estate agent with the key so we could have a look round. I persuaded The Other Half that it would be great fun to camp the night in the property's orchard, to get a real feel for the place.

It was fun but we passed rather a disturbed night. We hadn't appreciated that someone was renting the land to graze ponies on. They, curious at the sight of a tent suddenly appearing on their territory, came down the hill in the night and started sniffing around us. This caused Pez, the dog, to bark ferociously at the perceived threat so that the horses galloped back up the hill, bucking and squealing, only to repeat the game at intervals through the night.

Despite that, I loved the place. It wasn't exactly isolated, sitting just a mile from a small village with a pub and a Post Office, and there were no stunning mountain views from the property itself. But it was an awful lot of house and land for the money.

There were three large bedrooms and a box-room plus a bathroom big enough to hold a disco in. Downstairs was a big kitchen with a walk-in larder with raised slate slabs to keep stored food cool, a good-sized dining room and a nice sitting room with views over the fields belonging to the property.

The barn was huge and there was a cowshed and attached poultry house, plus two pigsties. The fields surrounded the house. One was big and flat enough to grow a good hay crop. The others were rougher but ideal grazing for ponies, sheep or goats.

Best of all, after The Patch, it was not overlooked at all. The nearest property was a small holiday cottage halfway up the access lane which was only occupied a few weeks of the year. Then down at the bottom of the track, a family and a single man had bought a plot of land between them and were each building themselves a home there. But they were only there at weekends and holiday and they clearly wouldn't be finished for a long time.

We discussed all the ins and outs on the drive back to Salisbury Plain. The Other Half wasn't keen on the separation, but he understood that the Army life wasn't for me. Perhaps he, too, thought that having our own space might perk things up a bit. So we put in an offer on the property, which was readily accepted. We were on our way to owning our own home.

In the meantime, my brother and Debs had finally found a

place they had both liked, not all that far away from our prospective home. Their offer had also been accepted so we would both be moving to the same part of the country. My brother, like my Other Half, was often posted away at sea, so Debs and I would be company for one another.

But, to quote an old saying which became the title of one of my favourite John Steinbeck novels, 'the best laid plans of mice and men' and all that.

The purchase of our future home, which was called Esgair, went through fairly smoothly and we were soon packing up our possessions and moving in. At least Ann and I, with Pez the dog and Taffy the pony, plus four cats we'd recently acquired, Eccles, Moriarty, Snoopy and Biggles, were moving in. The Other Half was moving a few of his possessions in; the rest would go into his new room at the Officers' Mess.

Things were not going half so well for my brother and sister-in-law. Although they'd never been all that close, my brother had decided to entrust our cousin, the judge's son, with handling the conveyancing for their property, which was called Pant Gwyn Mawr. Our cousin was a qualified solicitor and the transaction was a relatively straightforward one. Or should have been.

To cut a long and convoluted story short, the estate agent who was handling that sale was a rogue one. He'd been happily collecting deposits from several would-be buyers of the property, then had promptly disappeared with all the money. The fraud only came to light when my parents came to visit us, newly installed at Esgair, and we arranged to go with my brother and Debs to have a look at their new future home, Pant Gwyn Mawr.

Only there was another family already installed, having not long moved in. It seems our cousin had had his eye well and truly off the ball. So my brother and Debs lost not just their dream home but their deposit, too.

My brother and my cousin never spoke again and the

disastrous non-purchase marked the beginning of the end of my brother's marriage, although its death throes were long and protracted. He bought the first thing he could find on budget, only intending it to be a stop-gap. But once he'd bought it, he couldn't bring himself to sell it on. It wasn't what Debs wanted; not at all. It was in a small town, right on the main street, with no land. So no horses and no dream home.

But suddenly free of the shackles of Army life, I was feeling much happier. Weekends with The Other Half were going much better.

I was intent on doing the whole Good Life bit. I bought, in short order, a Jersey house cow, called Dusky, a pig, some chickens, ducks and geese, some goats, three border collie puppies, one of which went to be an Army dog with The Other Half, some more ponies, and took in a retired point-to-point horse, Monty, on loan. I also found myself a job on a local weekly paper in nearby Ammanford, so I was paying my way and putting food in the bowls and buckets of the growing menagerie.

Things were definitely better between me and The Other Half since putting some distance between us, and between me and Army life. It still wasn't unbridled passion but when he came for the weekends, we did things together – riding, going to local shows and events, walking the dogs – and generally being comfortable in one another's company.

We knew the Other Half was due a posting. We weren't quite expecting it to be two years in Northern Ireland, where The Troubles were still in full swing. Vague noises were made about whether or not I should go with him. If I'd found life on The Patch in Britain totally stultifying, I couldn't begin to imagine what it must be like living as, effectively, an occupying force in a partially hostile country.

Nor could I imagine what the anxiety would do to my mother if not just her son-in-law but her daughter as well was in Northern Ireland for two years. My mother had always been a professional worrier and forces' families were being targeted in the terror campaign.

When I moved to Esgair, I would sometimes meet up with her and my father at Newtown, which was halfway between our respective homes. About a two-hour drive for each of us. She always insisted that after we'd gone our separate ways, I should phone her to let her know I had arrived home safely. No mobile phones in those days, so I had to phone her from my house on the landline.

If I drove at my normal speed, which wasn't a lot more than the limit, and got home in good time, as soon as I phoned my mother and found her at home she would be saying I must have driven far too fast, it was far too dangerous, how could I have done it so quickly without taking unnecessary risks, etc, etc.

If I dawdled, staying well under the speed limit all the way home, I'd get the 'I've been so worried, I expected you home ages ago, I thought you were dead in a ditch somewhere.'

It was agreed, for the sake of all concerned, that I wouldn't go with The Other Half. I did visit, though, in dutiful wife mode. What a sobering experience that was.

I went over on the ferry from Liverpool and he met me at the port of Belfast. He had a small bungalow, out in the wilds, which was quite nice. But straight away I had to get used to the daily routine there of getting down on hands and knees to check under the car, as well as lifting the bonnet to peer inside, every time I drove it. Bomb attacks were not infrequent.

I also had to get used to never answering the door without knowing who was outside, and keeping a wary eye out to make sure I was never followed if I drove out to the cottage alone.

Above all I had to adapt to the sight of armed soldiers everywhere, and to the naked hate in the eyes of some civilians who looked at them – and at us. I was so glad I'd followed my instincts not to go with him on that posting.

Chapter Eleven
Jim'll Fix It

The Esgair years were good ones, by and large. It was hard work, as any kind of smallholding involving livestock always is. Especially when I was working full time as well.

I quite liked the newspaper I was working on and the people I worked with. It was my second attempt at finding a local paper. The first had been brief and unsuccessful. I found it hard to cope in an office where the chief reporter thought it acceptable to fart, loudly and frequently, by lifting one fat buttock from his chair and letting rip.

He also had a most peculiar way of running a news office. We were back in the Stone Age then, pre-digital. The office didn't even have electric typewriters. In fact, it was the only paper I'd ever heard of where reporters were expected to provide their own machines.

Most newspaper offices back then would have a large desk diary, the two A4 pages to a day type. Into this were written all the known events which would need covering. Everything from routine stuff like courts and council meetings, to things like the opening of some new building or amenity. It was the chief reporter's job to put initials next to each job so that everyone knew what they would be working on from one day to the next.

For reasons known best to himself, The Fat Farter always kept the office diary hidden away in a drawer of his desk. This meant braving the methane zone to get access to it and resulted in several newsworthy events being missed.

While working there, covering council and committee meetings for the local authority, I'd met a woman who worked on the Ammanford paper who tipped me off to a vacancy there, which I'd applied for successfully. A much more pleasant working environment, apart from the chain-smoking of the chief reporter who shared our office. If all the research about passive smoking is true, I've done well to last this long.

I survived the ravages of tobacco smoke, but my health did take a bit of a downturn whilst living at Esgair. Ironically, it was all the fault of the Good Life which was supposed to be so healthy.

As planned, I'd decided to take a hay crop off the flat field. The grass was good there and it would provide quite a few bales to see all the hungry mouths through the winter. I'd been lucky to meet and become good friends with a farming couple who lived about half a mile away. They kept a small herd of dairy cattle and, as the bottom had just dropped right out of the dairy business, the husband was working twelve-hour shifts at the local creamery to supplement the meagre income from the cows.

His name was John, and he was kind and helpful with his advice to me, a complete beginner in livestock management. He helped me find local contractors to come and mow my grass crop and later to bale it. I thought I'd be more eco-friendly and do some of the tedding – also known as wuffling, shaking up and turning the hay to let it aerate – by hand.

It was lovely hay, not dusty at all. But all hay is full of seeds and spores and pollens. It wasn't long before I was coughing, wheezing and struggling for breath.

Of course, all this would happen while I had my mother, Captain of the All-England International and Olympic Worrying Team, staying with me. As soon as she heard the crackling sounds my heaving chest was making she insisted I went to the doctor.

She was always paranoid about my chest, ever since I had nearly died of whooping cough as a baby. I'd been too young to be vaccinated. My brother had brought the illness back from school and apparently, had it not been for a new wonder drug they gave me, I would not have survived. It's why I'm in favour of vaccination and herd immunity.

The doc listened to my creaking lungs and pronounced that I had asthma. Asthma? I never expected that for a diagnosis, certainly not out of nowhere, as an adult. Oh well. At least, being allergic in origin, it was manageable. I just had to get used to carrying the infernal inhalers with me wherever I went and try to avoid allergens.

The doctor packed me off to the hospital for allergy tests. I knew I was quite tired, working possibly a bit too hard, so my body was probably feeling a bit feeble. It was clearly making its feelings felt. The nurse doing the allergy tests laughed when she saw the results and said it might be simpler to list what I wasn't showing up as allergic to.

The main culprits were grass pollen, dust and cats. Not ideal news, living the lifestyle I'd chosen.

Back to my kindly neighbours, John and his wife Brenda. They helped me to find someone to finish the tedding for me and soon my first hay crop was baled and stored in my barn. A good feeling.

I remember well what was to be neighbour John's last visit to my smallholding. He and Brenda had kindly come over to give me some advice on a problem I was having with my cow, Dusky. I was struck with how tired John looked. He was working far too hard.

While he was talking to me, he was rubbing his left arm, opening and closing his hand which he said had pins and needles. He didn't look well at all. I asked if he'd seen the doctor. He had, though not a brilliant one. He'd been given medication for indigestion.

Later that evening, someone from the village phoned me to

say could I go at once to be with Brenda because her husband had just collapsed and died on the yard in the middle of milking.

I jumped into my van and raced up there. What can you say? What can you do at a time like that? Poor John was still lying on the yard. Brenda was indoors, being comforted by the neighbour who had rung me. She had two small boys. All I could think of was how was she going to cope, on her own? She didn't even drive.

Words seemed empty, meaningless, so I opted for actions. There were twenty-odd cattle standing patiently in the parlour waiting to be milked. I could hand milk, but I had no idea how to use the machines. It would take me all night to hand milk that many. I got on the phone to summon up reinforcements who would know how to do it.

It was a terrible time. It affected all of us who knew them. Brenda decided to stay on, to carry on with the farm. I drove her to the shops when she needed to go and did what I could. I would take the two boys to the cinema of an evening, to give her some time to herself. We had great fun, the three of us, watching films I would never go and see by myself, without the excuse of small children to go with.

On those long dark winter evenings, we would both have an outside light on, over our back doors. It was all we could see of one another in the blackness of a country night. At a certain time each evening, first Brenda then I would turn our light off then on, three times in succession. Our way of saying, 'I'm here, I'm all right, are you?' Then we could each go to bed safe in the knowledge that we were there for one another.

I kept in touch with Brenda for forty years after I left Esgair. I would phone her every Christmas for a long chat. She died shortly before I wrote this book, so this was my first Christmas of not speaking to her. Perhaps if I repeat the outside light ritual, she might somehow be aware of it and respond.

It was while I was working at the paper in Ammanford that I had my infamous encounter with Jimmy Savile. The one which led me to say, long before anyone else did so publicly, that nothing which ever came to light about him – and I did mean nothing – would ever surprise me.

Lots of people will claim that it's easy to say stuff like that, with hindsight. Luckily, I'd said it to enough people back then to put it into time context. One person I said it to was a freelance journalist who worked occasionally for the Mirror. He contacted me the day before the story broke anywhere and said, 'You remember what you told me about Savile? Well, look out for the papers tomorrow.'

Ammanford is a small town in West Wales. Things that tend to happen there are fascinating to those from the Amman Valley, but hardly national newspaper headline-making events. Our offices were in one of the main streets, conveniently close to an excellent cake shop.

I gained the nickname, in the office, of Desperate Dan, after the cow pie eater from the Dandy comic. That was because I could eat my own bodyweight in the delicious sticky buns they sold without any effect on my boyish figure.

One of my regular duties there was the daily 'police calls'. That meant calling at the police station on the way in to work to find out what was going on. In those days the front desk was usually manned by a Uniform sergeant, a mine of information. If they didn't know about it, it probably hadn't happened.

At this particular station, I would often be seen by the Duty Inspector who was a nice, helpful man with a weakness for custard slices from the shop, so our chat would often be over tea and cake.

One day I answered a phone call at work which was from the owner of the nearby café to tell me that the famous DJ and television personality Jimmy Savile had just come in and ordered a drink. Savile was then the host of a show, Jim'll Fix It, helping children to make dreams come true.

I relayed this to our chain-smoking chief reporter, who asked me to go over and take a look to see if it was true and if so, to do a small piece for the paper about the visit from someone who was, back then, a famous celebrity and household name.

When I went over to the café, there were two men sitting at a nearby table. One was short and slight, with a woolly hat pulled low over his hair so it wasn't possible to see its colour. Savile had distinctively silvery hair which he wore quite long. The man also had a lot of bling, rings and the like, on his hands and fingers which was another trademark of Savile's but it was impossible to tell for sure who he was.

I introduced myself to the owner, behind the counter, and asked if he was sure about his visitor. He told me to hang on a minute then went over to the table. He came back grinning.

'I told him you said he looked like Jimmy Savile. He said you look like Lynsey de Paul.'

I crossed to the table and introduced myself to Jimmy. This was long before the knighthood. I asked if I could interview him for the local paper. He agreed but said he would prefer not to do so in a public place in case he was seen and recognised. He said his campervan was parked on a nearby car park and we could talk there in comfort and privacy.

Little did I know that I was about to spend about an hour with him in the infamous 'shag-wagon'. The other man – friend, roady, I never did find out which – discreetly disappeared leaving us alone together while I tried to stay out of Savile's clutches and concentrate on getting the interview I needed to write my article.

Did he sexually assault me?

No.

Did he behave inappropriately towards me?

Definitely, yes.

Why didn't you report him to the police?

Because this was the 70s. I was an adult. If I reported any

man whose hand strayed onto my thigh when it shouldn't have done, in those days, I would probably have been charged with wasting police time. It was the culture. And no, that doesn't mean I agreed with it.

So what was so different about him? What led me to say that nothing I heard about him later would surprise me?

He first tried to persuade me to visit him in London, promising he could open doors for me in my career. Somewhere in his Filofax collection, which apparently still exists, is an appointment he made for me. He called me Lesley Farmer when I told him I had a smallholding.

He was determined to get himself invited to my house if I couldn't be persuaded to go and see him in the Big City. I kept refusing, he kept asking. I said eventually that I had a large German Shepherd Dog who didn't take kindly to strangers.

He looked directly at me and said, in total seriousness, 'I've been trained in how to kill a dog with my bare hands.'

I knew he'd done training with the Marine Commandos. I believed him. I was in my mid-twenties, not a child, armed with a Biro and prepared to use it. Imagine what effect hearing something like that would have had on a young child, especially one who looked up to him.

So yes, I did believe everything which subsequently came out about him. I immediately phoned the Metropolitan Police, an officer working on Operation Yewtree as the investigation into him was called. I told him all about my own experiences with Savile. Lots of people were accused of jumping on the bandwagon at the time and making false claims with an eye to remuneration, the so-called Compensation Culture.

I assured him that all I was interested in doing is corroborating what the Met were already being told by younger people than I. I hoped that, me having been an adult at the time and confirming what was being said, might add some weight to other testimony.

It was a sign of the times that when I returned to the office and recounted the incident, the only comments were along the lines of 'Jim fixed it for you.'

Worse, when I told The Other Half what had happened, he merely laughed. Presumably it was some sort of affirmation that he had landed a wife who was sufficiently attractive to get groped by Jimmy.

Chapter Twelve
Blacks Making Nines

The Other Half was coming up for another posting. In the Army, soldiers and officers alike could get moved around every couple of years or so. Sometimes they'd stay in the same place but switch roles. Theoretically, officers could ask for specific postings, but it rarely happened that they would get the one they wanted. Unless they had some outstanding qualities. Which, sadly, The Other Half didn't, or so it seemed. He was proficient enough at his work but not noticeably brilliant at anything.

In those days, there was the possibility that he could be sent to some far-flung country. British troops were still present in Hong Kong, and there were postings to Belize. There were also an awful lot of postings, especially for the Artillery, in Germany with the British Army of the Rhine.

And that's where he was sent. He was going to be attached to the Divisional Headquarters in Lübbecke, in North Rhine-Westphalia, for two years. Naturally enough, he wanted me to go with him, otherwise we wouldn't be seeing a lot of one another.

My circumstances had recently changed when I'd had another of those 'seemed like a good idea at the time' moments.

I loved living at Esgair, surrounded by all the animals. I was quite happy with my job on the local paper at Ammanford.

Looking after animals can be perilous and I'm not sure I was believed when I had to phone in sick one time to say, with perfect honesty, that I had a concussion after a goat fell on my head.

My first milking female, Minnie Bannister, had been trotting along a raised wall which surrounded the orchard, just as I was bending down to collect up feed bowls. She decided to launch herself into the air, with that joyous spring and twist goats do so well, at the precise moment that I was standing up. The full force of her horned head and cloven hooves smacked me on the back of the skull and laid me full-length on the yard, seeing pretty coloured stars.

It wasn't always easy, juggling work and animals, especially once I was on my own again when Ann moved in with a boyfriend. We'd had some great laughs together, sharing house room. Especially when a local bachelor farmer had taken an interest in my lodger and had taken to calling round, sometimes bearing gifts, clearly trying to win her favours.

The trouble was he was fairly socially inept. One of the problems was that like many in that area of West Wales, Welsh was his first language. He was fluent in English but some of the subtleties of the Welsh were often lost in translation.

Another problem was that his main interest was sheep.

Now stop sniggering at once, dear reader. I don't mean it like that at all. That's just a foul rumour and calumny. I know lots of Welsh men who aren't interested in sheep in that way at all.

But this man – let's call him Dewi, although that wasn't his name – kept a small flock of sheep and did some buying and selling of them. He worked, like so many in the area, for the County Council highways department. But when he wasn't doing that, he was tending his sheep.

And there is absolutely nothing to laugh at in that sentence, either.

Because sheep were his passion – stop it, now – he

assumed that everyone else would be as fascinated as he was and, more importantly, that we would all understand what he was going on about.

Welsh translation note here - '*duw*' is the Welsh word for god but it gets used an awful lot in everyday speech and seems to be less blasphemous than in some other languages.

Dewi would come driving into the Esgair farmyard in his Ford Capri, at a time when that was quite a cool car to possess. He always managed to time his visits to when Ann and I were seeing to the various animals at the end of the day so we were a captive audience.

Another note, in case it's not universally used. Mart is the word for a livestock sale, market is where you would go to buy your fruit and veg.

'*Duw, duw,*' he would say. 'I've been to the mart today and blacks were making nines.'

Ann and I would risk an exchanged glance, trying not to giggle, neither of us having a clue what it meant so not knowing whether it was a good thing or a bad. Fortunately, '*duw, duw*' would fit either eventuality.

'*Duw, duw,*' I would say, shaking my head in wonderment. 'Nines, you say? Well, *duw, duw.*'

Another thing he did which would often reduce Ann and I to tears of hysterical laughter was to tell us jokes. These were clearly ones he knew in Welsh and would laboriously mentally translate. The first one he told us was moderately amusing so we laughed politely. It was the tale of an elderly spinster, hanging out her washing, when the line broke. The passing church minister kindly stopped to help her, then when he was finished, he told her, 'Now, Miss Jones, you can raise your skirts.'

She replied, '*Duw, duw,* and I only thought to give him a cup of tea.'

Okay, it wasn't going to win best joke at the Edinburgh Fringe or anything like that. But it was mildly amusing so we chuckled politely. This only encouraged him, however, so it became his party piece and he would recite it on almost every visit. Once we'd done the, 'Nines, you say? *Duw, duw,*' he'd launch into the tale of Miss Jones and her skirts, by which time Ann and I would be hanging on to one another howling with mirth before he'd even finished the opening lines.

Dewi's visits were nearly the death of me, quite literally, one time. Ann wasn't interested in his attentions and I was running out of ways to say '*duw, duw*' and sound convincingly interested. So we kept trying to come up with plausible excuses to get rid of him.

One time we said we were just going riding and he caught us out by saying he would come with us. He couldn't, it transpired, ride very well, despite his assurances. The horse I'd put him on, because he said he could ride, was a bit lively. He decided to settle his nerves by lighting a cigarette, but the sound of the match striking caused his mount to bolt. In the end he opted for leading it – a long way. But it didn't stop him coming calling.

I'd started doing some buying and selling of horses and ponies as a sideline. I'd not long bought in a young mare, unbroken, but who showed huge potential as a jumping pony for someone. Just for fun, she would regularly jump a five-barred gate out of her field then back in again and she was only small. She was a bright chestnut with a flaxen mane and tail so had inevitably gained the name of Goldilocks.

I hadn't yet ridden her. I hadn't even laid across her back in preparation, and she was a flighty little piece. I was just at the stage of leading her about with a bridle on and sometimes a saddle. Ann had her own pony mare, Basher, who had come from the same owners. She was staid and sensible and we'd broken her in easily enough.

On one of Dewi's visits, we were just about to go into the back hayfield, Ann riding Basher, me leading Goldie following her to familiarise her with little outings.

When Dewi saw us, he asked if we were just going out riding and, purely as a ruse to get rid of him, I said we were.

He was nothing if not the gentleman and gallantly legged me up onto my unbroken mount for the first time ever.

Luckily the gate to the hayfield was already open or I think we would probably have gone over it. Off Goldie and I went at high speed and totally out of control, with Ann following anxiously in our wake, probably thinking she would have a body to pick up.

It was a long way from my chosen method of backing a pony for the first time, and thank goodness for that long, thick flaxen mane, to which I gripped for dear life. I'm not quite sure how many circuits of the hayfield we did before we finally slowed down. But by the end of it, Goldie and I were starting to understand one another and we both lived to tell the tale.

Back to my brilliant idea, which turned out to be not quite so brilliant.

One day in the office, the woman at the next desk, the one who had first suggested the opening on the paper to me, pushed a newspaper across to me and asked if I'd seen the advert in the Situations Vacant column.

I hadn't, so I took a look at it. It was for someone to work in the Public Information Department of the Water Authority, editing the in-house newspaper. The salary was certainly attractive. Very attractive. So too, when I enquired further, were the fringe benefits.

For a start, you could work flexi-time. As long as you did the required number of hours per week, and logged them on your clocking in and out card, it was more or less up to you when you worked them. That made it easy for you to clock up enough hours to have three days off a week, from time to time. Ideal for balancing work with animal care.

Then there was a generous car purchase scheme, whereby you could get a brand new car with a reasonable loan arrangement. The manageable payments were deducted from your salary.

More in hope than anticipation, I decided to apply for it. I wasn't optimistic because although I had my qualification in journalism, this was a step outside what I'd been doing before.

Much to my surprise, I got the job.

It quickly became clear that with the new and longer commute, it was going to be difficult to juggle the job and the animals. But the money was good and, to begin with, the job was fine. So in consultation with The Other Half, who had not yet made the move to Germany, we decided to sell Esgair, buy a small cottage nearer to Brecon, where I would be working, and to downsize the animals, which would be the hardest part.

Naturally, I would be taking Pez the dog, plus the two border collies, Ajax and Jaffa. Sadly, the third dog, Brawdy, who had lived with The Other Half, had died young after managing to pick up poison somewhere on Salisbury Plain.

Of the horses, I managed to sell them all on to good homes, even the devilish Damien the Antichrist. I would be keeping just one, a young potential show hunter. His full name was Longden Wilhelm Rockefeller, known to his friends as Mannie, short for Chase Manhattan, after the Rockefeller connection. I found a place near to the new house where he could be kept at grass livery for the time being, as he was too young to do much of anything with just yet.

I kept a couple of the goats and some poultry and had runs made for them in the garden of the cottage which we bought at Talybont-on-Usk, as well as runs and kennels for the dogs.

It was small house, just a two up, two down, with a lean-to bathroom opening off the kitchen. Easy to maintain when I was out at work a lot of the time.

The garden was raised up high above the lane alongside it, which ran up to a reservoir in the mountains above. There were two large limekilns set into the wall, after which the cottage was named.

When we first took possession of it, we found an

unexpected bonus there, which nearly caused a riot with our dogs. The previous owner had allowed the local hunt to kennel its hounds in the limekilns and had failed to notify them that the property had been sold and they needed to move them out.

The Other Half went off to his new job in Germany. We spoke on the phone whenever we could. But I soon began to realise that the PR job was not the ideal match for me. My somewhat warped sense of humour often gets me into trouble as people take me the wrong way. In a role like that, it turned out to be a liability.

When you're in a situation where you're not happy, it's easy to look back on other scenarios and see them through the rose-tinted glasses of time. Was it so bad, being an Army wife, after all? Perhaps it would be different in a new country?

It could be a big adventure. Learn a new language, discover a new culture. We'd be able to visit my paternal family in Luxembourg. Go off on weekends and holidays discovering parts of Europe I'd never yet seen. My parents, even my Auntie, would love coming to visit us. Especially when I discovered that there was a regular, affordable Army family coach service which ran from London direct to a nearby garrison.

I told The Other Half I was thinking of coming out to join him. He was ecstatic. He enquired about married quarters and discovered we could have a brand new house away from The Patch, on a block of just four residences for officers and their families.

That didn't sound too bad.

Maybe it was time for another change, and to give married life another proper go.

Chapter Thirteen
Vorsicht! Bissiger hund

So far in my life I'd moved home three times, not counting the three moves I'd made with my parents when I was a small child.

When I'd moved from Esgair to the cottage near Brecon, my parents had sportingly come to help and had driven behind the trailer which was loaded with goats and poultry, in case any of the chickens decided to escape and fly out of the back on the journey.

It was going to be considerably more difficult to make the move to Germany on my own, since The Other Half was already over there. He was temporarily living in the Officers' Mess and whenever he phoned, he reported enthusiastically on the progress of the new house which was soon to be ours. It was the end of a small terrace of four, all being rented by the Army. As an end terrace, it had a reasonable amount of garden to the back and to the side.

I would be taking Pez, my German Shepherd Dog, with me, back to the land of his roots. I'd decided to let my new car go as I didn't want a right-hand drive in Germany. Also as I didn't know if I would find work there, I was worried about the payments on it. Luckily, as new as it was, it was simple to get rid of.

This meant Pez and I would be going out together, travelling by train and ferry to Zeebrugge, where The Other

Half would meet us and drive us to our new home.

In those days, before Britain joined the EU and with it the Passport for Pets scheme, it was quite a palaver to transport animals between Britain and the Continent. Britain had been rabies-free for many years, largely thanks to its strict quarantine rules and before the Channel Tunnel linked the two land-masses.

There was no quarantine going the other way, but you did need a raft of official paperwork, plus vaccination for rabies, two injections, some time apart. Some of these requirements were time-limited. Once you had your travel documents, they were only valid for three days, for presenting on arrival. If for any reason you missed your window of travel, you had to start the whole process over again.

My brother and Debs kindly said they would come and meet me at the railway station after the first leg of my journey, to help me safely on board. Pez was not the easiest of dogs for public transport as he was extremely protective of me and had been known to leap up and growl if anyone so much as looked at me the wrong way.

On the ferry, he would have to be put in a special kennel on the car deck and I would not be allowed contact with him for the duration of the crossing.

Because I would have my hands more than full with a big, strong dog, I would be travelling as light as possible, with just a small rucksack and a handbag. Everything else, my clothes, the furniture, all the rest, would be transported by a removals firm which did a lot of forces relocation moves so should theoretically know what they were doing.

Young Chase Manhattan, the horse, was going up to the RA Saddle Club on Salisbury Plain to be looked after until we found somewhere we could keep him in Germany, and a transporter to move him. He was still too young for me to do much with, other than handle him every day and get him used to being led round in a head-collar.

He'd been small when I bought him and rather pink. He was a colour known as rose grey. His steely grey coat was shot through with gingery bits giving the distinctive rosy colouring. I'd been worried he might not grow all that big.

I'd needed a vet visit at Esgair for one of the other horses and the vet in question turned out to be one who was a specialist in growth rate in horses. We had to walk past where Mannie was grazing to get to the other horse so I asked the vet, out of idle curiosity, what he thought of my new purchase.

He cast a critical eye over my little gangling yearling and pronounced, 'He's going to be big.'

He was right, of course. The weedy little colt eventually matured to a fine beast of just under seventeen hands, much bigger than I had imagined.

Sometimes, luck doesn't always run my way. My brother was always convinced there was a family curse on us all. I think everyone has bad luck from time to time. But perhaps between us we had more than most. Mannie certainly gave me a few heart-stopping moments when I decided it was time to get his tackle removed, to have him gelded.

Gentlemen readers will no doubt wince, but gelding a colt is not usually a big or a complex operation. The horse would simply be anaesthetised with an injection – Immobilon was the drug of choice in those days – snip, snip, all done, then another injection, of Revivon. In a surprisingly short time, the horse would be back on its feet, a bit wobbly and rather stiff, but happily grazing as if nothing had happened.

It was such a routine operation that it was, back then, frequently done out in the field, with few problems. If the horse did topple over a few times whilst recovering, it was probably less likely to injure itself than in a stable, unless it was extremely well padded.

There were a couple of problems with Immobilon. The first was it could happen that a vet might accidentally inject themselves with it if the horse was playing up and that was fatal, unless there was someone on the spot trained to give the antidote injection immediately. There had been cases where vets had died because the antidote was not close to hand or there was no one to administer it in time.

The other was that rarely – somewhere in the thousands or tens of, my vet told me – a horse's system would somehow ignore the Revivon and recirculate the Immobilon, effectively re-anaesthetising itself.

Guess who had one of the susceptible horses? And guess whose horse decided to put itself back under and fall into a ditch?

All very dramatic, but luckily, all was well in the end. We got him out of the ditch, the vet injected him again and it was as if nothing had happened.

That just left me with the question of what to do with the two remaining border collies, Ajax and Jaffa. Clearly, I couldn't make the train journey with three dogs in tow. It was going to be hard enough with one large one.

To my surprise, my brother and Debs offered to have Ajax. My brother liked animals but he was definitely more cat than dog. He had been bitten by a fair few dogs, even dogs which wouldn't normally bite anyone. So it was a doubly kind offer.

They were still living in their town-house so it was not ideal and both were working. But they did have a garden, and plenty of places to walk a dog including Pendine Sands, mile upon mile of sandy beach, so that should work out.

Then my parents said they would be delighted to have Jaffa, even if only until I got myself settled over there. My father had now retired from newspaper editing, although he still did a bit for the Church Times. He loved walking, always preferring to go to the pub for a pint on foot. He was still sacristan at the local church, too, and always walked there. In fact, since his retirement, he no longer had a car.

Jaffa was an easy and biddable dog, no trouble at all. She would love the walks and all the fuss and attention. More importantly, she was a very easy dog to handle. She was not likely to pull or knock my mother over as she was small and not very robust. She actually had to wear a sort of surgical corset under her dress for my wedding as she'd had a fall trying to put up a washing line and had broken a bone in her wrist and one in her back. She had recovered well enough but was wary of repeating the experience.

As for the cottage, we would rent it out initially and then decide whether or not to keep it or sell it. It was easy to find lodgers as it was handy for Brecon and for nearby Abergavenny and was a nice little place, with lovely views.

Remember my 'of mice and man' quote? I was all set to go. Just a couple of days off departure; my train seats, and Pez's place on board, all booked and paid for. All his official documents were issued and stamped. All my worldly goods, apart from a Snoopy sweatshirt and a pair of jeans which I would wear for the journey, were packed into containers aboard the removals van. Pez and I were camping out on the floor of the cottage, all set for the big day.

Then The Other Half rang to say there was a delay in taking possession of the brand new house. The infamous 'snagging' of a new build. There were a few things that needed to be put right before the Army were prepared to take it over. Not just ours, but the other three in the block.

I would either have to postpone travelling out – impossible, because of Pez's travel documents and incoming tenants wanting vacant possession – or be prepared to share his room in the Officers' Mess in the interim. That didn't sound all that appealing, but it seemed to be my only option.

Then it was the day of departure. Pez and I were up at the crack of dawn and got a lift to the station for the first train, from Brecon to Newport, from a kind friend.

Pez had travelled on buses and trains before and was usually good, as long as no one looked like a threat to me. But this was going to be a long and a potentially stressful journey for both of us so I'd taken the precaution of giving him a light sedative.

That was the reason I was grateful for my brother's and Debs' offer to come and help me on to the London train from Newport, as by that stage of the journey, the pill was going to be taking effect. Hefting a sleepy German Shepherd, who weighed nearly as much as I did, onto a train which made the briefest of stops might not be easy.

Because I had no idea of how he might react under such stress, and knowing that I would inevitably need a loo at some point on my journey, I'd carefully written out a card to hang round his neck if I had to leave him alone in a compartment while I nipped to the loo. I'd taken the precaution of writing it in several languages and had, in the process, learned my first useful German phrase: '*Vorsicht! Bissiger hund.*' The equivalent of Beware of the Dog. I was not remotely worried that anyone would try to steal him, although he was a stunning-looking dog with an excellent pedigree and was not castrated. Good luck to anyone who tried.

It was a wintry morning, cold and icy. When I got to Newport station and found the right platform for the London train, there was no sign of my brother and Debs, although time was getting on. My brother, like me, was usually punctual.

The stationmaster himself came walking down the platform and, seeing me and my massive dog, made straight for me.

For a moment, I had a horrible feeling that he was going to refuse to allow us to board, declaring Pez to be a danger to the public. I didn't have a Plan B for that scenario. If that was the case, I was well and truly stuffed, to put it mildly.

Instead, he told me that my brother had phoned him to say I was not to worry but he and Debs had had a minor road accident on the ice so they couldn't make it. Neither of them, nor Ajax, who was in the car with them, was hurt. Did I, in the circumstances, want him to help me lift my dog onto the train, asked the kind stationmaster.

Pez was already giving him 'that look' which was his way of telling a stranger, 'Take one step nearer to my mistress and you will die.' So I thanked him hurriedly and said as long as he ensured that the train didn't leave before we were safely on board, I would be able to manage.

The whole journey passed in something of a blur. We managed it. All the changes, me hefting a sleepy Pez on and off each train in succession. Finally we arrived at the Port of Dover, presenting all the paperwork and being escorted to the specially prepared kennel, where I had to leave Pez for the crossing. The kennel was inside a secure run so there was no chance of him getting out and rampaging round the car deck terrifying people. Mind you, by this time, he looked as if he was quite happy just to go to sleep.

The crossing at least gave me chance to use the facilities, stretch my legs and have something to eat without my dog in tow.

It was a long and tiring journey for all of us, including The Other Half, who was there at the docks waiting for us when we disembarked. I was supposed to get all of Pez's papers stamped to show that he had entered the country legally. But no one seemed remotely interested in a dog coming in from a rabies-free country. We had to wander about in the darkness, looking for some sort of a customs post where someone might kindly rubber stamp everything.

Eventually we did and we were once more on our way, a long drive through the night to our temporary home in the Officers' Mess. Twin beds, and narrow ones at that. Neither of us minded. There were no passionate reunions on the cards. We were all far too tired to do anything more than collapse into our respective places, Pez on the floor as close to me as he could get, and fall asleep.

Chapter Fourteen
Let There be Tripe

Normally, when you move house, your first priority is not tripe hunting. But you should know by now that nothing about me is ever normal, and in my circumstance, it was essential.

Pez had a pancreatic condition which had caused him endless problems before it was diagnosed after I'd had to take him to the veterinary hospital at Bristol for tests. It was a condition which could be managed either with medication or by dietary control.

Luckily for me, a change of diet did the trick. I was advised to feed him on tripe, preferably raw, straight from the slaughterhouse, and to add the occasional pig's pancreas to his bowl. I just hope you're not eating anything as you read this part!

It's a not uncommon condition in German Shepherds and a few other breeds. So much so that when I phoned the nearest abattoir to see if they could supply me, the man I spoke to immediately asked if I had a GSD with the runs.

If I didn't want to spend my days mopping the floor, not to mention washing down the walls, it was essential that I found myself a reliable source of tripe for him.

Military bases abroad are often set up so that forces' families don't need to have any contact at all with their new country, unless they chose to venture out into the big wide world. Most camps would have a NAAFI shop – Navy, Army and Air Force Institutes, which also provides leisure facilities such as clubs for the junior ranks.

We were now with a Divisional Headquarters rather than a regiment, so the set-up was slightly different, but we found a NAAFI shop not far away and luckily, they had tripe. We also discovered that there was an Army Saddle Club in the same garrison town, so not only would I be able to do some riding, there was somewhere for Mannie to live when we had him shipped over from the UK.

I quickly discovered that living a headquarters life, especially while we were still camping out in the Mess until our new house was finished and handed over, was one long social whirl. There were endless dinner nights and invitations to dine with the hierarchy. This included The Other Half's new immediate boss, a Brigadier, who was quite a character and had been on Olympic teams in two completely different disciplines.

His dinner parties were formal and legendary for the compulsory playing of charades. It was almost like some strange rite of passage for junior officers, to test their intellect. I was lucky. Call it second sight or what you will but I do sometimes seem to know what a person is thinking, if I concentrate hard enough. So as soon as someone gave us a two-word film, then held index fingers up to their head as horns, I instantly 'guessed' Apocalypse Now, which impressed all present.

My interest in films, and having been a member of the local film club when I lived at Esgair, also enabled me to contribute such hard to act out titles as 'The Effects of Gamma Rays on Man-in-the-moon Marigolds', which was always fun to watch and usually guaranteed to result in zero points for the opposite team.

At the weekends, there were tennis parties, Pimm's parties, any-excuse-to-get-sloshed parties. We were not all that far from the border with East Germany, long before reunification. I always used to reckon that all the Soviet forces would need to do would be to wait until late on a Sunday afternoon when all the Pimm's had been consumed then simply walk over the border. The chances of finding an officer sober enough to command his troops to stop them would have been slim indeed.

The Brigadier didn't greatly approve of such conduct from his officers. Allegedly, one night during an officers only dinner night – they were always worse when the ladies were not there to keep some sort of control over them – he sent the RMP (Royal Military Police) round to the Mess. They bundled the rather drunken officers into four-tonner trucks, drove them out into a forest in the middle of nowhere then instructed them to find their own way home, compliments of the Brigadier.

It was quite an effective way to make a point, but it didn't have any appreciable effect on the levels of drink, at least not that I noticed.

We were invited out often for dinner and drinks with other officers and their wives. My clothes had been delayed in transit, so another emergency shopping trip meant rushing round trying to find some suitable clothing for all this socialising. Apparently jeans and a Snoopy sweatshirt didn't quite cut it. Clothes shopping was not, and never has been, my thing.

All these invitations meant I had to spend time mingling with The Stepford Wives, desperately trying to find a suitably safe and inane topic of conversation with people with whom I seemed to have nothing in common. I remember one occasion where I stood in silent amazement listening to a debate between two wives about which NAAFI shop was better, based not on the commodities they sold but on the size of their trolleys.

Eventually, after a longer delay than anticipated, we were able to take possession of our brand new house, which was very nice. As was normal for houses in Germany, it had a large cellar, with a utility room for things like the washing machine and freezer.

Like all married quarters in those days, it came fully equipped and furnished with everything we could possibly need – except good taste. The stretch covers which were provided for our three-piece suite were so hideous they looked as if they were rejected camouflage covers. We could have draped them over tanks or artillery pieces to render them invisible from aircraft attack.

The Other Half had recently been promoted to Major and this, we discovered, entitled us to more items issued to us than for a lower rank. When I'd first moved into the married quarter at Bulford Camp, I'd discovered that as I was the wife of a lowly Lieutenant, we were only entitled to spare beds of two-foot-six wide. Useless me pointing out that my mother-in-law was a very well built woman. She had to wait until he was promoted to Captain and we could change the beds so she could get a comfy night's sleep when she visited.

As a Major, he could have a decanter, which made sense, as we were expected to entertain. But why the Ministry of Defence would decide that the issue of a soup ladle had to wait until the rank of Major was reached will forever remain one of life's mysteries to me.

Having our own house, well away from the main Patch, made our life more pleasant and we settled into some sort of contentment. Once we were installed, we had first Jaffa the dog then Mannie the horse brought over from the UK to complete our little family.

My parents visited and loved it. My mother came with her sister, my Auntie Ethel. I took them all round everywhere, showing them the sites. The lovely old half-timbered buildings in the small towns, the beautifully kept municipal parks, where the Germans loved to walk on a Sunday, all dressed in their finest.

They were amazed at the signs of prosperity, and at how well people were always turned out. My uncle came to visit with his sister-in-law. Both were widowed and had become good friends and companions after the loss of their respective spouses. They were surprised, out walking one day, when a German lady stopped them, trying to make them understand what she was saying. They eventually worked out that she was telling Bette that she had a ladder in her stockings, clearly horrified at the idea of anyone going out dressed like that.

I was certainly not one to want to live a segregated life of Brits only. I wanted to be able to go out and about independently to discover my new country. I had only a handful of German words at my disposal when I first moved there, apart from *Vorsicht! Bissiger hund*. The choice at my school, Stockport High School for Girls, had been between Latin and German. I wanted to do German. I was compelled to do Latin.

In the end, I didn't regret it. Latin is such a useful basis for grammar and modern languages. Though not a lot of use for doing your shopping.

So one of the first things I did was to sign myself up on a basic German course, provided by the Army for forces families.

Languages have never posed much of a problem to me. I pick them up readily enough, even if only to a superficial degree. Sums are a different matter altogether. Which is why my Sell the Pig travel memoirs series is a trilogy of five.

Having done the basic German course with no real difficulty, I then signed up for a more advanced one. Depending on what mark you got on this one, you could have the chance of going on an interpreter's course. That didn't interest me, but I did want to learn as much German as I could so I could enjoy my stay in the country more and feel independent going out exploring.

The trouble with this second course was that it was for military personnel as well as civilians, so it was delivered via military teaching methods. I'm a visual learner. I need to look at the words I'm saying for a better understanding. I need to know when and why *der, die, das* becomes *dem, die, das* or even *den, die, das.*

Because of learning Latin, I understand about nominative, vocative, accusative, and so on. But if I'm not allowed to know the why's and the when's, I get frustrated and struggle to comprehend.

Instead we had to sit there chanting in unison, '*Ich bin Stabsfeldwebel Peter West.*' Not a lot of use, since I could never see a practical application for when I might want to say, 'I am Staff Sergeant Peter West.'

Working in the language lab was lethal for someone with my lack of concentration. I'd listen through the earphones to the phrase I was meant to repeat, then dutifully say it back.

'Leider habe ich meinen Führerschein vergessen,' I repeated obediently.

'Unfortunately, I have forgotten my driving licence.'

A useful phrase, that. It could happen to anyone. Random stops by the police were not infrequent and we were supposed to carry with us at all times some form of identification, our driving licence and enough money to prove we were not vagrants. And to be able to pay the not infrequent on-the-spot fines for traffic offences which could make going shopping a costly affair, if you were not careful.

I said it a few times, as required, and had it lodged in my head. Unfortunately, they kept wanting me to repeat the phrase over and over, in different contexts. Imprinting, I believe it's called. And when that happens, if I have nothing to look at and focus on, my attention wanders and I start looking out of the window.

Oh, look, a squirrel. Awww how pretty.

That's a smart uniform. I wonder what regiment he is?

Oh dear, she really shouldn't be wearing that jacket with those trousers.

And all the time I'm repeating the phrase into the microphone without paying any attention to what I was saying.

Unfortunately, when I played back the recording to check for pronunciation and errors, I got an attack of the giggles when I heard that I had unconsciously changed the vital verb in the sentence to one which sounded similar but meant something completely different.

'*Leider habe ich meinen Führerschein gegessen,*' means 'Unfortunately I have eaten my driving licence.'

So it was not the ideal day on which to get stopped by a motorcycle policeman, parked at the side of the road, who brandished his red lollipop at me to pull me over. He asked if I spoke German then, when I said only a little, explained slowly and carefully that I had just gone through a radar trap whilst exceeding the speed limit so I would have to pay an on-the-spot fine.

The policeman was exceedingly tall and very fit-looking. He was clad from top to toe in motorbike leathers of green, black and white. That was distracting enough, but of course the next thing he asked me was for me to produce my driving licence.

I wondered how much it would augment my fine if I were to tell him that I had unfortunately eaten it.

Chapter Fifteen
Moving On

It was not at all the done thing for an officer's wife to go out to work. Mostly, they languished around drinking rather too much sherry and going to Wives' Clubs. That wasn't for me, at all. Especially as I didn't drink.

Fortunately for me, in our small social circle, there were two other officers' wives who did work and their occupation met with approval. Sue, a Captain's wife who lived at the other end of our block of four houses, was PA to the Brigadier, and another Major's wife was PA to the General. So when I found myself a few hours a week of clerical work in the same Headquarters building, for the Royal Engineers, it was not frowned upon too much. Just as well, as I hate to be inactive, and I like my independence. Especially financially.

Through a teacher in the forces' schools, whom I'd met whilst living in the Mess, I also became a Brownie Tawny Owl and a Guide Lieutenant. Despite never having wanted children of my own, I do enjoy working with them. Then handing them back to their parents.

Any group with children in it always has 'that one' and ours was Elizabeth. One day, at church parade, I was sitting next to her to keep a strict eye on her during the service. The church was very much High Church, with an impressive pulpit, from which the forces' chaplain, the Padre, was delivering his sermon.

My attention wandered for a fraction of a second. Then I saw Elizabeth, intrigued by the spectacle, solemnly starting to shin up the outside of the pulpit like a small monkey, to get a closer look at the Padre. I only just managed to catch hold of the hem of her Brownie uniform and tug her back down with a fiercely whispered, 'Elizabeth, get down and sit!'

To fill more of my time, I also got myself some teaching hours at the Saddle Club. As part of my duties would be taking rides out, it meant that I would get plenty of riding as well as instructing.

There was one little horse – not much bigger than a pony, really – at the Club who quickly caught my attention. For all the wrong reasons. His name was Aslan. He was a dun, a tawny colour like a lion, with almost black mane, tail, legs, ear tips and dorsal stripe. Well, his mane would have been that colour except it was hogged – removed with clippers, like a Skinhead. It was because he suffered with a condition called sweet-itch. It was a reaction to midge bites causing a flare-up almost like eczema which was incredibly itchy and hard to control.

Aslan was a cross between a Norwegian Fjord Pony and a Trakehner horse. This gave him the speed and temperament of a blood-horse with the strength and mischief of a pony.

Once a week a soldier from the Tank Regiment would come for a private jumping lesson, and he always asked for Aslan. I had to teach him. I think he must have been some sort of a masochist as I can't actually remember a single lesson when he didn't fall off.

Aslan was a very good jumper. Fast, bold and clever. He had a thing about combinations, though. Those are jumps with a number of elements, like a double or a treble. A fence, then another fence, one or two strides further on. He could jump them perfectly well and often would.

Sometimes, for no other reason than apparent malice, he would look as if he was going to take off, then at the very last possible second, he would bang the brakes on violently and duck to the side. With the combination of his short pony neck and no mane to grab hold of, it was difficult to stay put.

I swear it turned into a game Aslan was playing with this particular soldier, Gary. He would stop dead then appear to watch how far his rider could fly without him. Was that really a grin of triumph he gave when Gary flew off with such velocity in a one-stride double that he bounced, landed on the front pole of the second element and broke it?

How, I will never know, but Gary never seemed to injure himself and week after week, he would ask to ride Aslan and for me to teach him.

I could ride Aslan pretty much whenever I wanted to as, perhaps unsurprisingly, he wasn't popular with anyone other than Gary and he needed exercise. Lots of it. As The Other Half also rode a bit, we decided it might be a nice idea for him to get a horse of his own so he could ride out with me. He wasn't all that experienced so would need something of a schoolmaster which would look after him, especially as he wanted to start competing a bit.

The stables were managed by the wife of a Corporal who was the farrier for the club. She also did some work as a groom for a German show jumper, who was on the Olympic team. He did a bit of dealing in horses as a sideline. She told me he had something in which might suit The Other Half and went with me to see it.

German stabling in those days was different from much of what England had, although all that has changed now. The horses were kept in long indoor barns, with loose boxes, and there was always a wash-down area. The Germans seemed to be obsessed with washing their horses.

We met up with the show jumper, Uli, who told us that the horse, which was called Ali Baba, was all tacked up and ready for me to try, waiting for me in the wash-down area. He told us Ali was a six-year-old which had been bought for a lot of money to jump the big Puissance competitions as he could easily jump two metres. I gulped at hearing this – not with me on his back, I hoped! Ali was being sold for much less than the owners had paid for him because, although he certainly could jump big fences, he was basically a big lazy lump and only wanted to do three or four at a time rather than a full course. He was a German warmblood breed, a Westphalian.

The Germans do like big horses. There is no native pony breed in Germany so children often learn on big horses. Many of them start out by learning vaulting – mounted gymnastics.

As we walked into the wash-down, I got my first sight of Ali Baba. Or rather of his belly, as it seemed that the rest of him was towering above me. He was a whisker under eighteen hands, and I'm not very big. He also had great big legs like tree trunks which made him look even bigger and more formidable.

Uli suggested I first try him out in his flatwork arena as, like most German horses, he was well-schooled on the flat as well as over fences. Then if I liked him, I could take him into his jumping paddock and pop him over a few fences. I loved the casual way he said it.

I did like him on the flat. He was certainly lazy, but my electric seat produced a decent tune out of him. The brakes were excellent and it was clear that he wasn't going to be the sort to scare a novice rider, as long as they didn't ask too much from him. Pressed too hard, he had been known to rear and that was certainly not funny on a horse already that big. Left to his own devices, he was quite happy just to trundle along, unless you rattled him up a bit. A perfect schoolmaster. Time to try him over some fences.

Uli opened the gate into his jumping paddock and laughed when he saw my face turn green. He was an international Grand Prix rider, regularly competing over fences of five foot three inches (1.6 metres), with spreads up to two metres (six foot six) and his practice jumps reflected that. I'd never jumped anything that size in my life.

He obligingly said he'd lower some of them a bit for me. They still looked huge.

German riders almost always wore long spurs, well before they were a thing in Britain. As I'd no idea what I was going to be riding, I hadn't even put on my short, blunt Prince of Wales spurs. Nor was I carrying a whip. I shortened my stirrups to jumping length then sat up off the big horse's back and had a couple of canters round, trying to rev him up a bit into jumping mode.

He jumped everything I put him at, with minimum effort. He was one of those horses who did a lot of grunting when he jumped, as if it was all too much trouble for him. I was pleased with what he'd done. He would definitely be safe enough for The Other Half.

But Uli wasn't satisfied. He said the horse was lazy and could, and should, do much better than that, so he said he'd get on him and get a better tune out of him. Uli was short, no bigger than me, but stockily built. He looked like a pea on a drum on the chestnut, probably as I had done. But he was wearing long rowelled spurs and had a jumping whip.

He did a couple of circuits, firing the big beast up, then pointed him at one of the jumps he hadn't lowered for me, an enormous triple bar. I'd never before seen so many poles in one jump.

The ground literally shook under our feet as the big horse came thundering in to the fence. Then he just seemed to get completely flustered by Uli's signals and barely took off at all, just crashing through the whole thing, sending poles flying in all directions.

Luckily, Uli was nothing if not sporting. Laughing loudly, he cantered back up to us and skidded to a halt. Then he leapt off, throwing the reins at me, admitting the horse had gone better for me and telling me that I should definitely buy him.

Buy him we did, and we had a lot of fun competing with him in show jumping and hunter trials. He gave The Other Half a lot of confidence, carrying him safely and steadily round the kind of courses he wanted to jump.

The only problem with him was his sheer size. With him in the trailer, our poor car struggled to pull him. Eventually we decided to move him on. We did a part-exchange at the Saddle Club. Aslan became mine, together with a cash balance. They took Ali Baba, on the understanding that The Other Half could ride him whenever he wanted to and had the time.

Between the riding, me working, and us being able to visit other countries, spending our holidays doing trips to France, Italy, Austria, Switzerland and Luxembourg, our time there was good.

I went off to Berlin one long weekend on a Wives' Club trip. I usually avoided Wives' Club like the plague, but it was useful for such things. One of the other working wives, who was a good laugh, was going as well, so I knew it would be far from dull. We went on the train, through the Berlin Corridor, as it was long before the Wall came down.

It was an exciting and an eye-opening trip. As we crossed the border into East Germany, the train doors were locked and chained to prevent anyone getting off, or on. There was much ceremony at the station as documents were shown by officers from the East and the West. An Eastern guard walked the length of the train, on the outside. We were briefed that we had to hold our passports up to the window but mustn't make any facial expression and mustn't on any account turn over more than two pages in response to gestures from the guard.

It was a time of heightened tension between East and West – I forget the reasons now – but I didn't dare so much as look at the guard. As soon as someone tells me not to laugh, under any circumstances, I am consumed with a desire to giggle.

We were only in Berlin for a couple of days but we were determined to pack in as much as we possibly could, with sleep as a low priority. We went on a guided coach tour of East and West, passing Checkpoint Charlie and seeing the contrast in living standards on each side of the Wall.

We did another guided tour of the night-life hotspots of the west. We saw half-naked ladies fire-eating on roller-skates while they stripped off fully – yes really – and I was proposed to in one club by an American Mormon.

We walked a good length of the famous Kurfürstendamm shopping avenue, gazing in at the windows at things I could certainly never afford. Most of them I wouldn't have wanted anyway. It was far too ostentatious for my modest tastes. When would I wear a mink-lined trench coat?

But, as ever, we weren't going to be staying in one place for very long. Julius-Brecht-Strasse, Lübbecke, had been our home for two years now, so we were due another posting. We were staying in Germany, being sent to Dortmund, where The Other Half was to become a Battery Commander (BC) with a regiment at Napier Barracks.

It was time to pack up our things and our animals, Pez and Jaffa the dogs, Aslan and Mannie the horses, and make the two-hour journey to our new home.

We'd been married nearly ten years by now, but had only lived together for six of them. Still, you would have thought that I would have known better than to blithely set off following The Other Half in convoy, in days long before mobile phones or satnavs.

He'd shown before that he was hopeless leading the way, always forgetting to check, after lights, junctions or other obstacles, that I still had him in sight.

It was easy enough for me to get myself to Dortmund, simply by following the signs on the motorway. But I'd not yet seen our new home and had no idea where it was. All I knew was that our house was in Leimkuhle, Limekiln, road, the same name as our cottage near Brecon.

Again, by following the signs, I managed to find my way to the barracks to ask at the Guardroom where my new house was. They kindly directed me to the right road and I soon spotted The Other Half's car on a driveway.

So I finally arrived, tired, stressed and more than a little grumpy at having been abandoned. Not an entirely auspicious start to our new posting.

Chapter Sixteen

Walkies!

The following morning, feeling slightly more refreshed and in a bit better humour, I got my first look, in daylight, at my new home and surroundings.

The house was a three-storey semi-detached with four bedrooms – we got an additional one now as befitted a Major - plus the customary large cellar. There was a small patch of grass behind a hedge forming a front garden of sorts, then a reasonable-sized rear garden which was fenced so it would be ideal for the dogs to relax in.

It was situated in a road of properties rented to the military. Not all Army, as our neighbours on one side were a teacher in the BFES (British Forces Education Services, Germany), his wife and their three sons.

The house was a short distance away from the Barracks where The Other Half was to be based. There were plenty of places within the Barracks to go for long walks with the dogs.

To gain access, you had to park up and go into the guardroom to sign yourself in, and then repeat the same procedure when you left. Security was tight as, with the situation in Northern Ireland always volatile, terrorist attacks were always a possibility.

There was a tram service from the end of the road we were living in which went into Dortmund town centre. So it would be easy to go exploring on public transport, without risking more speeding fines.

Best of all, the Barracks had its own Saddle Club, where Aslan and Mannie were now safely installed, so I could visit them every day, ride out on Aslan and start leading Mannie out with us so he got more experience. I'd recently backed him (ridden him for the first time) and he was getting going quite nicely. For a time before we had left our previous home, I'd kept him and Aslan in a German Saddle Club which was nearer than the military one so more convenient.

I'd nearly had a nasty accident in the indoor school with young Mannie. I was just getting on him when it was all still a bit new to him. The rules of indoor school use are strict and universal. Nobody is allowed to open a door without first knocking and waiting for permission to enter.

For some reason, another club member either forgot the rule or for some reason thought that the school was empty. I was just swinging my leg carefully over Mannie's back when she flung the big heavy sliding door open, making a lot of noise.

Mannie leapt into the air then exploded into a huge buck. I did a fairly graceful flight through the air and landed on my back against the solid wooden kick boards which ran round the walls. The young girl had the grace to be apologetic.

It hurt. A lot. I afterwards discovered I had torn an intercostal muscle, the ones between your ribs. I can tell you confidently that it's impossible to breathe without expanding your rib cage and therefore pulling the already damaged muscle. But it healed fast enough. I've always had a super-fast metabolism and therefore good recovery times.

Life in the German club had been a bit of a culture shock. The feeding regime there was that every horse was fed on whole oats. And they all got the same measure, regardless of their size. Oats have a reputation for making horses lively, and Aslan didn't need any help on that score. Surprisingly, after a couple of days of him pinging and bucking whenever I rode him, he settled down and was no different to his normal explosive self.

The German club gave us a chance to mix more with local people and to get to know a bit more about the German way of life. Most of their methods with horses were certainly different to what I was used to from living in Britain. For one thing they hardly ever rode out. All the exercising was done in an indoor school or occasionally in a fenced outdoor arena. Some of the horses were never turned out to grass at all, which was an alien concept to me.

Once a year, the club organised a ride out, all on the road. They marched along in solemn procession to take a glass of something with a club official at his house. The palaver they made about it! No one was allowed to go on it unless they had been having lessons indoors for two years and had been certified as capable. I declined the offer to go along.

I rode out all the time, often by myself. Despite having defective brakes, Aslan was uncomplicated in that he was not afraid of anything. Except frogs, as I discovered one time when I was standing him in a clay-based pond to help his windgalls, the equine equivalent of swollen ankles. A frog swam towards us, croaking noisily, and Aslan teleported himself into a vertical take-off which nearly dumped me in the dirty water.

Nothing much else bothered him. He had a pet mouse in his box which would come and eat next to him in the manger, happily sharing his oats.

One day when I was riding him out through a built-up area, we had to pass under a railway bridge where workman had things like oxyacetylene torches, spitting sparks everywhere. They didn't even notice us approaching, so didn't switch off.

I was fairly certain that Aslan wouldn't mind, and he didn't. Which was just as well as at the same time we had to pass them, a train decided to rumble past directly over his head. That didn't bother him, either.

The German club had a Hungarian riding master who

thought Aslan was one of the most dangerous things he'd ever seen. He clearly thought I was insane to ride him. He had a fabulous horse called Tarragona, Tarax for short, which I was honoured to be able to ride occasionally.

He wasn't the only one to think Aslan was lethal. Some of the Life Guards, with their distinctive black ceremonial horses, were stationed nearby. They were part of the Household Cavalry, the ones seen on parades in London.

In Germany they would compete in the various competitions I went to. Often, little Aslan and I would find ourselves in the same winning line-up, although lower down, as one big black in particular, Black Chief, ridden by a Corporal of Horse, the Life Guards' equivalent to a sergeant.

He was an accomplished rider, seemingly afraid of nothing, so I was surprised when he commented to me, as we made a lap of honour together one time, that he couldn't understand why I rode anything as mad as Aslan.

Then one day a friend showed me a video of the two of us jumping in a competition, me and Aslan. No wonder he had gained the nickname of Whiz-wham from the Pony Club kids who knew him. It was terrifying to watch. There was no functioning stop mechanism, just a bit of steering if I was lucky. If he didn't bang on the brakes, he was very hard to beat as he hardly ever had a pole down and he was always fast.

On this particular video, he'd taken exception to the second part of a combination. He'd done his infamous trick of actually appearing to take off before changing his mind then putting his front feet back down and ducking out to the side. I was ingloriously ejected right into the middle of the fence, scattering poles in all directions. To add insult to injury, because I still had hold of the reins, the bridle came right off and Aslan disappeared without me so I was unable to finish the course.

As the wife of a BC (Battery Commander), I was supposed to

take an active part in the Wives' Club and to help to organise events, especially when the menfolk were away on exercise. It was my idea of hell.

The Colonel's wife, married to The Other Half's commanding officer, popped round occasionally to remind me of my wifely duties regarding Wives' Club. With great self-control, I refrained from setting Pez onto her.

I didn't care for her husband, which posed a problem, since our paths were bound to cross, often. The first time we met, at some sort of function in the Officers' Mess, one his opening comments to me was, 'I don't like dogs.'

He clearly knew I had two of them, so it was an intentionally provocative comment. Never having been one to hold my tongue, I merely smiled as sweetly as I could and replied, 'I generally find that I don't get on too well with people who don't like dogs.'

My dogs were important to me. I enjoyed their company. The Other Half and I decided to set up a small, modest dog training club in the camp. I'd always competed a bit with Pez in obedience competitions, at low level. He'd won me a stack of rosettes. But he was getting on a bit now, no longer able to do the things he could previously do.

His digestive problems were being kept in order with plenty of tripe from the NAAFI shop. Some of the women who worked on the tills there were married to men in The Other Half's Battery. Before I explained that the tripe was for a dog, I think they thought that was all I ever gave the poor BC to eat.

Jaffa was a good little dog, very easy to handle, always biddable. She made an ideal dog to demonstrate the basic techniques needed to encourage people to get going in our club.

Dog training back then was different to today. It was all a bit regimented, lots of marching about doing heel work. Dog were routinely in check-chain collars. It was not intentionally barbaric, just the way things had always been done.

Then along came Barbara Woodhouse with her tweed skirt, sensible shoes and trademark cry of 'walkies', who changed things forever. She was the first of the self-styled dog whisperers, with a programme on television. She was well-meaning but definitely eccentric and possibly not as good as she claimed to be. She was also supposed to be a horse whisperer. She claimed to be able to control horses by blowing up their noses.

The big annual equestrian event for the military in Germany was the Rhine Army Summer Show, in which I regularly competed, and The Other Half had a go at a few classes. We'd always go for the two days of the show and stay over.

One year Barbara Woodhouse was appearing to give a dog training demonstration in the main ring. It hadn't gone according to plan and when I queued next to her for the loos, I noticed that her hands were covered in sticking plaster which had apparently been the result of a bulldog taking exception to her training methods.

Later on, I was riding a horse called Chieftain, which we were later to buy, trying to get from one arena to the other. He could be exceedingly stubborn and if he didn't want to go somewhere, he would show his disapproval by rearing and waving his front legs in the air.

As soon as he started to plant his big hooves and to get stroppy, Barbara Woodhouse, who was not far away and had seen his resistance, began striding towards us, with the determination of a heat-seeking missile.

Chieftain was not a big horse, being only about 15.2 hands. But he was part draught, solidly built and named after the Chieftain tank for that very reason. Seeing him right up on his hind legs, with his soup-plate feet flailing in the breeze, Ms Woodhouse suddenly remembered an important appointment elsewhere and left us to get on with it.

Our dog club, on the old airstrip inside the camp, was

somewhere between the two methods. No silly words but no rough stuff either. Just a bit of socialising between the dogs and a way of getting people to ask a bit more from their canine companions.

One person who joined the group was a man called Marty who, together with his wife Pat, ran the NAAFI club on the camp. They had a young boxer dog called Toyah.

Rumours circulated that Marty was a bit of a hard man. Ex-Parachute Regiment, later SAS (Special Air Service) and recently retired from there as a WO1, Warrant Officer First Class. The SAS are the ones with the motto 'Who Dares Wins' and are sometimes nicknamed the Hereford Hell's Angels. That's because their barracks are in Hereford and they're a pretty wild lot. They're the ones who get sent in on the most dangerous and dirtiest missions. The ones no one else would touch with a bargepole.

Marty certainly didn't look anything special. He wasn't tall, perhaps five feet eight, and not well built. There was a certain wiriness about him which could perhaps conceal strength. Jimmy Savile was of a similar build and, up close and personal, I had certainly sensed a latent menace about him.

The thing which convinced me that it was probably true was that The Other Half's Commanding Officer was the brother of the CO of the regiment which Marty would have served with, if he was who he led people to believe he was.

It would have taken a special sort of idiot to put themselves at such risk of their cover being blown in those circumstances.

Marty may well have been the legendary hard man. But when it came to his dog, he was a great, big softy. One evening he didn't turn up for dog club as usual. Instead his wife came to tell me that their dog, Toyah, had a sore paw. Nothing serious, just enough to stop her from attending. She said Marty was worried about her and too upset to come and present his excuses himself.

I rather liked that. That a man who would kill someone without question just because he was told to do so would be affected like that by even a minor injury to his dog.

Chapter Seventeen
War Breaks Out

As I was going to be spending a lot of time at the Saddle Club, and because I enjoy working with young people, it was inevitable that I should become involved with its Pony Club branch.

I had become friendly with the local Padre's daughter and, as she rode, she used to come and ride out with me often, she on young Mannie, me on Aslan. Another of life's bizarre coincidences. Not only had we met the daughter before back in Bulford Camp days, the new sergeant in charge of the Saddle Club, who joined shortly after we arrived, turned out to be none other than the Staff Sergeant from Larkhill days, on Salisbury Plain. So he also knew Mannie and was happy to ride him a bit and to compete on him in his first ever hunter trial.

I never intended to keep Mannie for myself. He was bought as an investment, with future sale in mind. Now he was going nicely, the wife of another officer we had met asked if she could have him on loan for a time. It suited both of us ideally. It gave her something nice to ride while she was looking for something of her own to buy and she was an experienced and sensible enough rider to bring on a young horse.

Although I'd ridden and worked with horses for many years, off and on, I'd never bothered with any of the BHS (British Horse Society) exams. That's because I had encountered many BHS qualified instructors who I wouldn't leave in charge of a hamster, let alone a stable full of horses. But if I was going to be doing more in the Pony Club, especially as I was quickly elevated to DC (District Commissioner) I thought it might be prudent to get a piece of paper to wave.

It was no great honour to be chosen as DC. It was like the old military joke: 'I need a volunteer. That man there! Step forward'. I didn't mind. It was fun working with the kids and going off to shows with them almost every weekend.

Fun was always my watchword. I competed for fun. If I won, great, if not, never mind, there would be other days. That's always the philosophy I taught to those Pony Club children. Apart from anything, it helped stop them turning into the sort of poisonous little brats who took it out on their ponies when they didn't win. Probably because we went with that attitude we always came back with a stack of rosettes and trophies between us, having had a wonderful time.

A Colonel from a regiment different to The Other Half's was the Stables Officer for the Saddle Club and he decided to get involved one day. Instead of their usual team talk from me – have fun, take care, be nice to your ponies and yourself, and remember to be sporting, win or lose – they got a great long lecture about winning for the honour of the Club, the Regiment and goodness knows who else. The Queen, probably. It went on, and on, until their little eyes were glazed over.

I had never before seen those kids ride so badly. They did unheard of things, like forget the course in the show jumping, getting themselves eliminated for taking the wrong route, sometimes jumping a fence from the wrong direction. They had some really good ponies between them and should, as usual, have wiped the floor with the opposition. They came home with not a single rosette between them, looking so dispirited it broke my heart.

Luckily, when the next competition came around, the Colonel was away on exercise so I was back in *chef d'equipe* mode. I walked the courses with them, to make sure they knew exactly what they were doing and where to go. I told them they were all brilliant and were going to have a fabulous time. Above all, I told them winning wasn't important. Taking part and enjoying themselves was what it was all about.

Off they went, all smiles, full of confidence once more. They slaughtered the opposition but, as they'd been taught, were gracious in victory, congratulating those they had beaten. They were thrilled to be once more adorning the sun visors in the lorry with all their rosettes for the homeward bound journey.

I decided, that in order to get my official piece of paper as a BHSAI (British Horse Society Assistant Instructor), the first rung on the ladder, I would go back to the UK for a brief visit to make sure I was up to date on exam technique. I subscribed to a couple of horsey magazines so I trawled the advert pages for a suitable training centre.

My trip was to be for a few weeks, sufficient to get updated training and take the required exams, which happened over two separate days. One was for the teaching element, the other for the stable management.

I chose a riding centre with a good reputation and two Olympic team members on its list of instructors. My chosen dates coincided with The Other Half being away on exercise so I needed to sort out cover for the horses, which was easy.

We only had the one dog, Jaffa, by this time. Dear old Pez, my companion of more than ten years, had had to be put to sleep when, as with many older German Shepherds, his rear end started to go. The loss of mobility was tricky with a dog of his size, but I managed. But when he could no longer stand up and wag his tail to greet me when I came home, I knew he was no longer enjoying his life. A kind Army vet gave him the gentle way out and he slipped away quietly as I stood beside him stroking his black and golden fur for one last time.

To my surprise, my father volunteered to come over to

Germany to babysit Jaffa for me whilst I was away. I'd never got on particularly well with my father and it was unusual for him to go out of his way to do anything for me. But he was missing Jaffa. He'd enjoyed having her to stay and it would be an ideal set-up for him, living in our married quarter. He and Jaffa could toddle round to the barracks every day and head for the Officers' Mess where he could have a pint or three, on The Other Half's tab, before walking back home again.

So with The Other Half off playing soldiers, all my animals being taken care of, and my father in charge of videotaping all the episodes of The Professionals which I would miss, I went off to England to do my training and take my exams. I was driving myself over in the sporty little Renault 5 which I'd bought since moving to Germany.

As I was now in my thirties with horses of my own, I had decided to go as a student, rather than the other option of working student. This meant I was not required to do any yard work, unless I had a burning desire to do so. It also meant I would be living in a rather nice, well-equipped chalet, sharing with one other mature student, rather than the more bunkhouse type of working student accommodation.

Coincidences, remember? It turned out that my roomy was a PA to an Army officer and had encountered The Other Half at some point in her travels.

The update course was great fun. I knew the basics of everything I would need for the exam. I just needed sharpening up and polishing to conform to what the examiners were looking for. Whenever I had been critical of BHS instructors in the past, people had told me it was sour grapes because I wasn't one. So now I was set on becoming one, then I could see if my opinions were justified.

In those days, anyone could put in for the BHSAI exam with no previous qualifications. This was quite dangerous as it meant there was no vetting process of the candidates who were turning up at the exam centres. It's not a particularly high standard of riding, but you do need to have a bit of control over horses both show jumping and going cross country. It was possibly slightly more dangerous in the teaching phase as candidates would be in charge of giving a lesson to a small class and would often be too ambitious to be safe. The rules were later changed so that candidates had to pass the two earlier exams, Stages I and II, before putting in for their AI. But I was able to leapfrog both those exams at the time.

At the training centre, we humble students were not often taught by the Olympians, a brother and sister. They spent most of their time teaching the more lucrative private clients. Sometimes the sister taught us and her lessons were always excellent, stretching us to the maximum.

I remember being taught by her over gymnastic grids – several jumps in a row with varying stride lengths between them. I was riding one of the old plodders who was not showing a lot of enthusiasm until fired up by my famous electric seat. She announced that I rode like a terrier, for the way I chased him up over those fences. I think it was a compliment.

Sometimes their mother taught us and she had an, erm, how to put it tactfully? An interesting and unique way of teaching. She was not opposed to giving you a thump in the solar plexus if she thought you were slouching. She was also inclined to forget when she was supposed to be teaching us, so we could end up endlessly warming up our mounts in the indoor school waiting for an instructor who never materialised.

The brother was responsible for much of the management of the centre. He was tall, slim, attractive, especially in his breeches and boots. Let's call him CB. One day I was lying on my bed in the chalet revising from a book when he knocked and came in. The central heating had been playing up and he asked if he could feel the heat of the radiators to see if they needed bleeding.

I was mortified. I had just been washing my smalls and had

them spread out the full length of the radiators, where he was busily rummaging to sort out the problem.

I've always had an overdeveloped sense of humour and mischief. It gets me into a lot of trouble, but it's just who I am.

All of us students ate our meals together in a communal dining room. That evening, at supper time, I waited until there was a lull in the conversation then just dropped into it airily, 'CB touched my knickers.'

For the exam, which I was taking over two days at a centre near Preston, I stayed the nights with my Auntie Ethel in St Helens, which wasn't far away. She was always pleased to see me and there was always a large and nourishing hot meal on the table. Doubly welcome because the exam days were cold and icy.

Because of the conditions, we couldn't jump outside, so had to do extra show jumping in the indoor school. Part of the exam was the ride and lead, riding one horse whilst leading another alongside it. This was having to be done in a somewhat frozen outdoor arena because the lanes around, where it would usually take place, were not safe enough, given the weather conditions.

It was something I did as routine every day with Aslan and Mannie, so I just got on with it without much prompting from the examiner. When I brought my horses to a halt, I was feeling reasonably confident. It had gone well, no problems with either horse, correct hand signals given at appropriate times, nothing dangerous. Or so I thought.

I was surprised, therefore, when the examiner asked me if I knew what I'd just done. Obviously I did, as it was so routine to me. Then I realised what she meant. Whoops! I'd done the whole exercise perfectly – but on the wrong side of the 'road'. I had the led horse on my right, instead of my left, to be on the inside. I was so used to doing it in Germany I had been on autopilot.

Luckily, when I explained and pointed her towards my left-hand drive car on the car park, she made allowances and I passed all sections of the exam.

So now it was off back 'home' to Germany, armed with my certificates to wave. My horses had been fine and were looking well. Jaffa had had a great time with her 'grandad', although The Other Half's bar tab had probably taken a battering. I drove my father to where he could catch the forces' family coach back to London, then a train back home to Stockport.

It was time to start trying to be a good Army wife once more, although it appealed even less after a break away. Especially Wives' Club.

But a couple of things were about to happen which would change the course of my future once more.

In April 1982, the Falklands War broke out. British troops were hastily sent to the South Atlantic, though not, at that stage, anyone from The Other Half's Battery. It was a brief but bloody conflict, lasting ten weeks and costing the lives of two hundred and fifty-five British military personnel. Even after the conflict, a military presence was to continue there up to the present day, to hold the territory against Argentina.

The next future event was an impending visit from The Queen to the area. I have never been a monarchist. I was prepared, with gritted teeth and fingers crossed, to raise a glass in the inevitable loyal toasts at dinner nights in the Mess when the chorus for the Artillery was always, 'The Queen. Our Captain General.'

But when I heard that wives would be expected to attend a dinner night in the royal presence for which the required dress code was ball-gowns and long gloves, I was already mentally writing a note from my mum to say I wouldn't be able to come out to play that night.

Chapter Eighteen
Closing Ranks

Marty the boxer owner was about to prove himself to be a good friend and a useful ally. I'd sold Mannie to a regiment which had grey ceremonial horses. They had a big and an important parade coming up when one of the greys would be ridden to take the salute. Unfortunately, the usual one was lame and they didn't have anything suitable for the task.

Mannie was still slightly pink but he was getting more grey as he matured. He was now just six, still a youngster, but all his early education of going out and about with Aslan was paying off. He was a remarkably calm and well-behaved young horse, not easily worried by anything.

Every year, all the Pony Club branches from different Army bases would come together for the annual summer camp, which took place on Sennelager Ranges. I went along as an instructor, taking Aslan with me for escorting rides out. The Padre's daughter came with me one year and I lent her Mannie for the week as it was excellent education for him. It got him noticed.

When I put the word out that he was for sale, I was contacted by the Regiment who were looking for another ceremonial grey. They asked a lot of questions about him which I answered as frankly as I could. They wanted to know if they could have him vetted, which was standard procedure and to be expected, and if they could also keep him on a week's trial.

I had no reason to object to either. They were reasonable requests. As far as I knew, he was sound and healthy. He'd had one brief period of lameness previously. There was nothing much to show a reason for it so I'd taken him to a German vet who was a specialist in foot lameness, and that's where Mannie's problem seemed to stem from.

I went with a German woman I'd become friendly with. She kept her horse at the same Saddle Club and we often rode out together. She was married to a British soldier and her English was fluent. My German, by this stage, was adequate for most everyday situations, but I wanted to be absolutely certain of understanding everything the vet told me. Apart from anything, his consultation fee was expensive so I wanted to make the most of it.

My German friend, Petra, did a lot of Competitive Trail Riding with her horse. That's endurance riding, over set distances of anything from ten to one hundred miles. The horse is subject to stringent veterinary examination throughout the duration of a ride. It's not sufficient to complete the distance in a set time. The horse must pass all veterinary examinations in the process. Depending on the rules of the different organisations, this includes a final vetting up to two hours after the end of the competition, when horses may well have stiffened up, without great care.

Aslan and I did a bit of Trail Riding, reasonably successfully, but both of us much preferred jumping. The training discipline was good, though, so we would often ride out with Petra.

Mannie's examination by the German vet was long and meticulous and included X-rays. At the end of it all, he explained carefully, with Petra interpreting where I needed to be sure of meaning, that it appeared that the lameness stemmed from some bruising inside the front foot. Not from underneath, as in an injury from impact with the ground, but across the front of the foot.

I told him that Mannie was notorious for banging a front foot against his stable door when he thought it was about time someone came to feed him. The vet agreed that was the most likely cause, gave us some anti-inflammatories and we went on our way, happy that there was nothing serious going on. And in fact the injury did settle down and showed no signs of recurring.

I drove Mannie down to the other Regiment's stables where not one but two Army vets were waiting to examine him. One was British Army, the other on secondment from the US Army. They gave him an extremely thorough going over.

A common test for lameness in horses during a vetting is called the flexion test. Each foot in turn is raised and held up, flexed as far as the joint will allow and held there for about a minute. Then the horse is immediately asked to trot away. It's a pretty reliable way of showing up any kind of lameness. Mannie passed with flying colours.

I agreed to them keeping him on trial for a week as I appreciated they needed to be absolutely sure he would fit the bill before paying for him. His role for the upcoming parade would be to stand as still as possible whilst the officer riding him took a salute. As the officer would therefore only have one hand free to hold the reins, it was essential to have a horse which didn't fidget.

In addition, the Regiment in question was an armoured one and there would be tanks on parade, rumbling past not far away from where Mannie would be standing. It was asking a lot of such a young horse to take it all in his stride and behave. Hence my agreeing to a week's trial.

At the end of the week, the Stables Officer phoned to say Mannie had passed every test they subjected him to with flying colours and they would be delighted to buy him, at the full asking price.

He phoned me again not long after to say that the parade

had passed off brilliantly and everyone had been impressed by Mannie's behaviour. Or rather Chase's, as they preferred that part of his name, Chase Manhattan, so now referred to him as Chase. He had stood like a rock as if watching tanks roll past under his nose had been a part of his life since the day he was born.

It was a different story a few short months later when the same officer phoned me again. From the outset, his voice and manner were different. Accusatory. Chase, he informed me, was now lame and their vet had diagnosed navicular disease.

More correctly a syndrome than a disease, navicular is a progressive, degenerative condition of a bone, the navicular bone (so called because it's said to be boat-shaped) in one, or more usually, both front feet. It also affects the bursa and the deep digital flexor tendon. It's one of the conditions which usually shows up on a flexion test. It hadn't shown up when Mannie was examined by the two vets.

I pointed this out, to which the officer replied that I must have doped him up to the eyeballs so that he passed the vetting.

Still remaining patient and polite, I asked him why, in that case, as they'd had him on a trial for a week – long enough for any such medication to have worn off – it had taken so long for any lameness to show up.

His response to that was so ridiculous that I laughed out loud. He said the only other explanation was that either I'd been visiting the stables in secret to top up his medication. Or that the horse had been denerved and I hadn't declared it.

Denerving, sometimes called nerving, or neurectomy, was once a fairly common practice in horses. Nerves were surgically severed to stop pain being felt so the horse ceased to be lame. The blindingly obvious rebuttal to his argument is why would a horse which had undergone neurectomy go lame, since it had lost the ability to feel the pain in the affected area?

Added to that, with security measures on high alert at all barracks, how could I possibly have slipped into the stables when no one was there to administer medication without first signing in at the guardroom? The officer only needed to check the signing in book for either my signature or the registration number of either my or The Other Half's car to show that that suggestion was also ludicrous. I'd also have had to be doing that not just for the trial week, but daily for the weeks and months since then, if lameness had only just become apparent.

We were going nowhere fast. My parting shot was that I had sold the horse in good faith, subject to vetting and trial, both of which he had passed. In view of the time elapsed since then, the possibility that the condition had arisen since they had bought him could not be ruled out. Therefore I was not prepared to take him back and refund their money.

It was during all of this that I discovered the real meaning of the phrase 'close ranks'. It was also an opportunity to find out who my true friends were, those who would stand by me without question.

The situation quickly became nasty. The Other Half's former boss, the Brigadier, became involved. He was an accepted equestrian expert as one of his Olympic disciplines was eventing. He got on to The Other Half and suggested forcefully that I should admit the deceit, refund the money and take Mannie back.

I was appalled when The Other Half actually suggested this to me. No question of him considering that I might actually be telling the truth and that Mannie was sound as a bell at the time of the sale and only became lame later on because of something which might have happened to him in the intervening months.

I was still in contact with my old friend from our former Saddle Club, whose husband was a farrier. He told me, off the record, that the farrier at the stables where Mannie was now kept had a bad reputation. Allegedly one of his party tricks when shoeing horses was to drive a nail in with a single hammer blow.

No self-respecting farrier would ever dream of doing such a

thing because of the possibility of error resulting in catastrophic damage. When shoeing horses, the nail is driven into the insensitive, horny part of the hoof, rather like the human fingernail. It's done with careful, repeated taps of the hammer to ensure at all times that it's going in correctly. Because extremely sensitive tissue lies close behind it. Imagine driving a darning needle into your nail with one savage thrust and getting it wrong.

But he stressed that it was off the record. He could never say as much in public, for fear of his career. Ranks were closing. Even The Other Half wanted me simply to roll over and admit something I hadn't done, for the sake of keeping the peace.

I decided I needed to consult a lawyer, a German one, to be sure of their impartiality when it came to the British military. But I wasn't confident that my German would be up to the complexities of such a complicated issue. Someone told me that Marty, the boxer owner, spoke German up to interpreter standard and suggested I ask for his help.

Remember our recurring theme of coincidences in life being stranger than those in fiction? As soon as I'd heard Marty speak for the first time, I'd recognised his accent. Bulawayo. The part of the former Rhodesia where my father had spent much of his wartime service with the RAF. Marty was not his real name but a nickname. Something to do with where he had been educated, in Cape Town, South Africa.

I asked him if he would consider helping me by translating at the lawyer's. I was worried that, being ex-Army and reliant on the Army for his current job, he, too, would close ranks, suggest I let the matter drop and cut my losses. Instead he said he would be delighted to help in any way he could and would certainly come with me to translate. He warned me he knew little about horses so might not know any technical equine words. Luckily I did.

He even offered to drive me there. I knew he had a sedate

automatic saloon car, in which he, the wife and the boxer dog would appear sometimes for training. When he turned up to collect me to go to the lawyer's office, I was astonished to see him at the wheel of a brand new, low-slung, sleek white Mazda RX7 sports car.

I've always been fiercely independent. Done my own thing. Looked after myself. Suddenly, probably for the first time in my life, it actually felt nice to have someone in my corner, helping me, believing in me and above all, not judging me. Stepping outside the ranks which appeared to be closing all around me.

On the short drive to my appointment, I discovered there was much more to Marty than met the eye. Although he was modest and didn't boast, I'm a journalist by training so I'm quite good at getting people to talk about themselves. I discovered that German was only one of several languages in which he was fluent, including Russian. I could imagine that skills like those would open up all sorts of possibilities for where he could usefully be deployed.

I knew enough to know that Special Forces like he had been were often the most unlikely looking people. The best cover for any operative was always to be able to say something as close to the truth as possible so there was no possibility of forgetting a cover story.

Close up, I judged him to be about five foot eight, slim to medium build, and probably in his late forties. Getting on for twenty years older than I was at the time. His hair was grey but still thick and plentiful and he wore a thickly bristling moustache, typical of many people's ideas of a Sergeant Major, fuelled by films like Zulu.

His accent was pronounced at times. More so, I discovered when I got to know him better, after he'd had a can of Foster's or a bottle of German lager, which was about all he ever drank. I could easily imagine him walking into even a Republican stronghold pub in Belfast, announcing himself to be British

Special Forces on a spying mission, and having people laugh in his face.

He was kind, courteous and extremely helpful. So was the lawyer. He felt I had nothing to worry about, and nothing to answer. Letters were exchanged. The whole matter died a death. But it left a lot of bad feeling behind it. I, in particular, felt betrayed by the system. And particularly by a husband who hadn't had the bottle to stand up for me.

I asked Marty if there was anything I could do for him in exchange for all his help, as I believe in that good old currency of 'swapsies', returning a favour with a favour.

There was, as it happened, he told me. He'd always wanted to learn to ride and never had done. Could I possibly teach him?

As we had, by now, bought Chieftain, the steady big tank of a horse who was ideal for novices, I said I would be delighted to do so. We made an appointment for his first lesson.

Chapter Nineteen
Stop Right There

If the impending royal visit alone had not been enough to make me want to run for the hills, my experience with the Mannie Affair certainly did. I'd always felt myself to be a square peg in a round hole as far as Army life was concerned. Now I didn't even feel as if I was on the same peg-board.

The Officers' Wives were more unbearable than ever, to me. At the prospect of being able to eat at the same table as the monarch, all the time wearing their long gloves, they were as clucky and excited as chickens in a poultry house who had got the whiff of a fox. They were fussing about which ball-gown to buy. Some were talking about getting more than one, so they could decide at the last minute which one to wear.

There was much rivalry but also collusion. No one wanted to run the mortifying risk of turning up on the night to find that someone else was wearing the exact same creation.

I was bored witless by the whole thing. I hate shopping at the best of times, especially for clothes. The most excited I'd ever got on a shopping trip was in a sports shop when I discovered that a pair of leather-seated corduroy breeches which I'd been lusting after for some time had been drastically reduced in the sale, in my exact size.

I loved those breeches. They fitted like a second skin, looking as if they had been spray-painted on. They were a flattering and forgiving shade of deep bottle green. I wore them until the suede strappings up the insides of the legs and round the seat had worn away to nothing and the corduroy had completely lost its pile.

But flouncy ballgowns and long gloves? Elaborate hairdos and make-up? Not my thing at all. Coupled with which, there were all sorts of wild rumours circulating about the domestic arrangements necessary for accommodating the royal presence. The Queen would be staying in the home of some high-up military personage. We heard talk of such things as a new lavatory having to be installed since the royal bottom couldn't possibly sit where other more mortal cheeks had reposed.

Even if only a fraction of these stories were true, they offended my principles, such as they were.

Since the Mannie Affair, I was giving quite a few people a wide berth. As one of them was the Stable Sergeant at the Saddle Club, it made things awkward. I'd discovered that he'd been saying all sorts of things about Mannie and his supposed lameness to the enemy, as I now regarded anyone who had stood against me in the matter. I noted that he had carefully omitted to mention that it had been him who had ridden Mannie round his first-ever hunter trial course, and done quite well. He could hardly claim to have done that on a horse he alleged had been lame.

I was spending more time now with Marty as he was keen to ride as often as was possible. We'd bought Chieftain for The Other Half but there were frequently days when he couldn't ride him. As well as his Army role, he was a rugby referee and a hockey umpire, so he often went to matches, even when not officiating. This meant Chieftain could get some exercise with me giving Marty lessons on him then, as he progressed, taking him out hacking.

The Germans had an extremely sensible system for horse owners and riders. In Germany you were, quite rightly, responsible for all of your actions and their consequences, with no grey areas. If you had children who were minors, you were responsible for theirs also. It applied as much to riding horses as to driving cars.

When families first arrived to live in Germany, they were presented with a pack, a sort of 'Idiot's Guide to German Living.' The joke always was that in Germany, anything not compulsory was prohibited. It was a bit like that but, far from being oppressive, it actually made it very easy for everyone to live in harmony as they all knew the rules and mostly abided by them.

You weren't allowed bonfires, nor to hang out your washing, on Sundays. Not for religious reasons, but because it might be some people's only day off. They wouldn't want to inhale your smelly smoke, nor have to look at your smalls blowing in the breeze while they relaxed in their garden on the only day on which they could do so.

Each householder was responsible for clearing snow from their front door right to the extremity of their property, including the pavement outside. And the rules about when you had to put out and bring in your dustbins were clearly set out and had to be followed on pain of hefty fines.

So it was no surprise to discover that, before you could ride out on horseback, you had first to go to the local municipal offices, armed with proof of third-party insurance, to register yourself and each horse you proposed hacking out on. You were then issued with bright yellow plastic ID tags, with an identifying number on them. These were fixed to the sides of the horse's bridle and had to be displayed at all times when not on your own land. That way, if you should be inconsiderate enough as to gallop across a farmer's field, damaging crops or frightening livestock, and they saw you, your number would be reported. Then you would get the dreaded knock on the door from a fearsome German policeman.

Marty was a surprisingly good pupil. He had excellent natural balance and fast reflexes. I suppose he would have needed both for being parachuted into hostile territory. He was fit and his legs, in particular, were strong. All that yomping the Paras are famous for.

Above all, because of his military training, he could take instruction and correction. If he was attempting something beyond his capabilities, he would at least listen when I checked him. It didn't take him long to reach a standard where he could quite safely hack out with me in walk, trot and canter and pop over a small log on the way if we happened to encounter one.

He was pleasant company to ride with. Getting him to talk about himself was not always easy. But it's a known phenomenon that riding horses banishes inhibitions, helping people to relax and encouraging them to feel comfortable enough to talk. It's all to do with the particular gait of the horse, especially in walk, moving the rider's seat and trunk in such a way as to stimulate the central nervous system.

One day as we let the horses amble along on a long rein, coming back from a ride down a narrow track, Chieftain slightly behind and to the side of Aslan, Marty was smiling dreamily to himself. When I turned and caught his eye, he suddenly announced that he thought that he was falling in love with me.

Whoa! Stop right there. Where did that come from? Patiently, not wanting to hurt his feelings, I explained that that was another well-known phenomenon. Riding pupils regularly fell in love with their instructors. I certainly did, at sweet sixteen, on my first residential riding holiday.

It's the same as patients falling for their nurses, physiotherapists, doctors and so on. Powerful feelings, seemingly genuine, but not usually so. Once the patient is discharged, the plaster cast is removed, or a new instructor comes on the scene, such feelings are generally seen in perspective. I decided to ignore it and carry on as normal.

Because of the increasing malaise I was feeling, I'd discussed with The Other Half that it might, once more, be time for me to pack up my things and go and live an independent life back in the UK. To my surprise, he didn't appear to put up much resistance. Perhaps he realised I was more of a liability than an asset to his career.

His Colonel's wife continued to call on me at random, exhorting me to do more with the Battery Wives as would befit a BC's wife. Go round and kiss newborn babies. Ugh, please. I've never been fond of babies, which is half the reason I never wanted any. Puppies and kittens, yes. Babies, no.

I was also supposed to organise functions for them when the men were away. I didn't like this welfare aspect of my supposed role. I particularly disliked being sent round to inform one wife that her husband had been injured while away on exercise and was in hospital. I didn't feel equipped to do it. I had no guidance on what to say and what to omit, plus I didn't feel I knew enough about what was wrong with him, nor how serious it was.

I was even less enthusiastic than I was before about Wives' Club as I now had another job, one which was right up my street. The BFG – that's British Forces in Germany, nothing to do with giants, friendly or otherwise - has its own newspaper, called Sixth Sense. As it's a forces' paper, it's more of a PR sheet than a newspaper in the true sense of the word.

They were advertising for an editorial assistant. I applied and was accepted. The editor seemed amazed to have found someone with my qualifications and experience readily available.

The role was not taxing. We were past the days of hot metal presses now so all the subbing I would be doing was on clean proofs printed from a computer, or directly on the screen. The compositors no longer dealt with metal hammered into place for the page matrix, covered in printer's ink for a proof to be run off. Instead they made up pages on a clean work station, using a sharp knife to cut strips of paper to fit the proposed layout.

As well as subbing, I would also be writing headlines and

rewriting copy which came in from untrained local correspondents and often needed knocking into shape before it was readable.

The offices were in the small town of Körbecke, on the banks of the Möhne reservoir, scene of the famous Dambusters raid in 1943. The bouncing bombs developed by Barnes Wallis breached the dam causing catastrophic flooding which killed an estimated sixteen hundred civilians.

There's now a pleasant open park on the banks of the reservoir. I used to take a packed lunch with me and eat it there, enjoying the peace and quiet.

Working there kept me out of the way of Wives' Club and the like. But it didn't stop the hankering to leave all of it behind me.

The Other Half and I started discussing what sort of a property we should get next, to give ourselves a base in the UK and, preferably, give me a means to make a living. Now I had my BHS certificates, I suggested looking at riding centres, possibly residential holiday places. I was still getting some horsey magazines on subscription so I started flicking through them to see what sort of thing was on offer.

We'd sold the cottage in Brecon and instead bought a small place in Devon, which I had never seen. The in-laws were living in it, paying us some rent. They were quite happy to buy it from us, so we wouldn't have a chain. Added to which, we had sold the smallholding, Esgair, for much more than we'd paid for it as Welsh property prices had been booming at the time, so we had money for a decent-sized deposit.

We had become good friends with our neighbours, the BFES teacher and his wife. I'd taught the whole family to ride and helped them to buy their first family pony, a stocky little Haflinger which was suitable for any of them to manage.

They started coming with us to competitions so we spent a lot of time together. When we told them of our plans to buy a riding centre for me to run, back in UK, we were both more than a bit surprised when they received the news with great excitement. They said, if we were interested, they would like to buy into the dream – and the business – and help to run it.

We'd not considered the idea of a partnership, but it opened up more possibilities. With their input, we could get a bigger place, already a going concern, which would give us a head start.

Best of all, the husband, Eddie, as a teacher, had quite a bit of holiday time coming up and volunteered to go back to UK to look at a few, to give us a starting point for discussion.

Wales was still the best value for money on property with the land necessary for a riding centre. From the magazines, we picked out a couple of likely-looking ones. One was in North Wales, on the Llŷn Peninsula. The other was in West Wales, the part which has been variously called Carmarthenshire and part of Dyfed, because of local government boundary changes.

Our old friend coincidence. Remember him? Here he is again. The West Wales centre was one I knew. When I'd been living at Esgair, Ann the lodger had got a job there. I'd driven her there for her interview, and had gone back with her some time later when the owners had fallen on hard times and not been able to pay her wages. They wanted her to work on, promising to pay her in full once things picked up. I helped her to point out that she needed fuel for the moped I'd lent her to get to work, not to mention money for food, clothing and everyday needs.

The place was called, in Welsh, Ffynnonlas, but those enterprising owners had given it the English translation of Blue Well. Nearer the top, alphabetically, in any listing. Always a good point when considering advertising. And easier for non-native speakers to pronounce.

It had ten acres of land plus grazing rights for horses on several hundred acres of moorland right outside its gates. It had been trading up until quite recently and was being sold with ten horses plus all their tack and a lot of other equipment, including bunk beds and bedding for children's riding holidays.

Eddie was as eager to go and look at it as we were to have his report on its current state and potential viability.

Chapter Twenty
Angel Song

Eddie arrived back from his mission upbeat and excited. As soon as we could find the time, we all sat down together to listen to his feedback.

He didn't think the place on the Llŷn would be ideal for various reasons which made sense when he explained them. But he was full of enthusiasm for Blue Well. He was not enough of an expert to comment on the horses included with the sale, other than to say that they all looked in good condition.

He gave a sound assessment of the commercial potential of the place. I hadn't seen all that much of it on my previous visits there. My one abiding memory was of some small wooden structure which looked like a poultry house but was supposedly where the children who came on holiday used to sleep, with its grand name of 'the bunkhouse'.

The main problem initially was going to be accommodation. We hadn't been thinking of a place big enough for seven of us as well as future residential customers. Blue Well had a small old cottage with one bedroom upstairs and another in a ground-floor extension. Built on to the side of the house was another extension with three rooms of bunk-beds, giving sleeping room for eight children in total. There was a separate self-contained Portakabin-type unit, furnished as a self-contained chalet. None of it was yet high-class living, but it was functional and could be improved.

The best part of it, Eddie told us, was a converted barn, separate from the main house, which was done out as the dining room, with big, solid wooden refectory tables. Large picture windows gave a lovely view right down the valley and over the forest which adjoined the property. There was a good-sized kitchen on the side for preparing meals for visitors. There was also an outside shower block, two residential caravans and a wooden hut, like a scout hut, which was used as a games room for the children in the evenings when it was too wet to be outside.

It all sounded ideal. The next stage would be for me and The Other Half to go next, to have a look and see what we thought of it. He had some leave coming up and Marty and Pat kindly offered to look after Jaffa while we went away.

Jaffa got on with almost everyone and was fine with Toyah the boxer. I had always thought she got on with absolutely everyone but there was an international incident one time which took me by surprise.

There was a problem with our telephone on one occasion so I'd called the phone company and asked for an engineer to come round and sort it. Punctuality was always a big thing in Germany. The appointment was made for eight o'clock one morning and the man rang the doorbell at ten to. Jaffa was sitting quietly in her basket in the hall. She never bothered about visitors, so I didn't give it a second thought.

The man knew he was coming to a British household so he began the formalities in passable English. He saw Jaffa sitting looking at him so he asked me, in English, if she bit. I said she didn't, because she never had.

But he switched back to German as he held his hand out to her so Jaffa, with an expression of outrage on her face, snapped at him. Luckily she didn't make contact and the man was kind enough to accept my explanation of her not being used to hearing German spoken in the house. I hadn't realised my dog was a racist.

The Other Half and I travelled back to the UK in his car, having dropped Jaffa off with Marty and Pat. We took the ferry from Zeebrugge then drove to Wales where we had booked into an hotel.

Blue Well was much as I had remembered it from my visits there with Ann, just more run down and a bit shabbier round the edges than the picture I had held in my head since then. The couple who owned it were in their sixties, he in particular no longer in brilliant health, which is why they were selling.

Their niece and her husband had been helping them with the place but it was all now too much for the older couple, despite the help. They were keen to sell up and move down off the mountain to somewhere more manageable.

The riding centre nestled in a hollow on top of a windswept plateau, about a thousand feet above sea level. Not all that high, but when the wind came from due east, there was nothing much higher between it and Siberia, judging by the icy blasts which could descend.

From a riding point of view, it didn't get much more perfect. From the gate to the property, you rode out onto several hundred acres of open moorland then, just a few yards by road in either direction took you onto yet more open spaces or into Brechfa Forest, more than sixteen thousand acres, with endless tracks to be explored.

I was anxious to cast an eye over the horses which we would be buying, if we decided to have the place. There were ten, and some of the names were familiar to me from when Ann had worked there. Most were cobs or cob crosses, ideal for the work and the terrain.

Sula, a Welsh Cob cross Thoroughbred, had always been the ride leader's horse and the owners warned me that he could be lively, not suitable for any but the most experienced rider. What they didn't tell me at the time but I found out the hard way was that he was prone to bolting. He had in the past, when going full steam ahead, jumped a cattle grid on one occasion and a five-barred gate on another, with a rider on board.

Barney, Danny, Lucci, Winston and Wags were all strong weight-carriers, easy for anyone to ride. Gloss was another Thoroughbred cross but safe and sensible. Jay was an Arab-cross-Appaloosa, though he looked nothing like either breed, and was one of the safest, steadiest horses I'd ever met.

The other two were a small pony mare, Mouse, and her yearling colt, Kismet. In addition, there was a piebald cob, CJ, who was on loan.

It's never happened to me before or since, and I have no idea why it did, because I would never mistreat any animal. But for some reason, CJ took an instant dislike to me on sight. If he saw me approaching him, in a field or out on the moor, he would attack me. He never did it to anyone else, only me. Naturally enough, when we did decide to buy Blue Well, he was one of the first to have to go, back to his owners. It was too embarrassing in front of customers for me to have to run and hide from one of the horses.

Because after looking all round the place and spending some time with the owners, we did decide to buy. It seemed perfect for what we had in mind. We went away to crunch a few numbers, to sort out some finances, then we put an offer in with the agent, which was accepted.

We'd decided that for the time being, the purchase would be in our names, then we could create the business to include Eddie and his family. At that point we could sort everything out on paper to make sure it was all watertight and there were no misunderstandings.

Back to Germany we went, full of hope and anticipation. Jaffa was, as ever, delighted to see us back, although she had been well looked after. She would, of course, have to go into quarantine for six months on her return to the UK as the Passport for Pets scheme had still not yet been brought in.

When, a couple of days later, Eddie and his wife knocked

on our door and asked if we could talk, we could tell, just by their faces, that it was not going to be good news.

They were sorry but the wife had got cold feet. She had three sons to think about, with all the consequent changes of school to organise. In addition, it was not certain that Eddie would be able to walk straight into a job. Most schools in Wales required all teachers, of whatever subject, to have at least a basic grasp of the Welsh language and Eddie had none. There were too many imponderables, too big a risk to take. They were out before they were even in.

It was a blow to our plans, but not a catastrophic one. We had been forging ahead to make the purchase in our own joint names so, for the moment, it changed nothing. And an unexpected solution was about to present itself.

Naturally enough, riding out with Marty and chatting to him about our plans, I'd mentioned we were now without partners. He said nothing, except a few sympathetic words.

Later on, he turned up on our doorstep to talk to me and The Other Half. He wondered if he and his wife could be considered as replacement business partners. He could offer services in teaching all sorts of outdoor survival skills and had worked in Outward Bound-type centres in Cornwall. She was a cordon bleu cook.

It was completely unexpected. And it opened up a whole new range of marketing opportunities for the centre. It was ideally placed for all kinds of outdoor survival training, which could run effectively alongside the equestrian side of things. Moreover, the basic accommodation was no problem as that could be part of the learning experience.

We didn't immediately strike up a new partnership. It was a case of once bitten, twice shy on that score. But the suggestion certainly gave us food for thought. New plans were made. It was all starting to get very exciting.

Then a couple of things happened which would effectively shift the goalposts.

The first, although it shouldn't have been unexpected, was that The Other Half was informed that he and his Battery would soon be heading to the South Atlantic for a tour of duty in the Falkland Islands.

The second was less predictable and still to come.

While The Other Half was doing all that was necessary to get him and his Battery to the Falklands, I was busy planning the logistics of moving me and the horses to Blue Well, once the sale was completed. First, I needed to find a nice quarantine kennels for Jaffa's long incarceration.

One of the advantages of working on the Forces' paper was that people were coming in and out of the office all the time to place adverts. On one occasion when I was talking to someone at the front desk, the man who came in to place an advert was a licensed pet carrier, who transported animals from the UK and back to quarantine kennels there.

He gave me several useful tips on how to pick a good one and a few names to try. One was in Gloucestershire and the carrier told me it seemed good. I gave them a ring and spoke to a nice lady who asked all about 'doggy's' needs and preference. She told me they had radio piped to the kennels for company during the day and that if 'doggy' had to be there over Christmas, there was a special dog-friendly Christmas dinner on offer.

It sounded ideal. I booked it and sent the deposit, then arranged the carrier. The sooner Jaffa went, the sooner I could get her back again once I was installed at Blue Well.

As the married quarter was fully furnished, we hadn't brought much of our own furniture out to Germany. Most had been left in storage, so I would need to arrange for that to be delivered to Blue Well once I was there.

There was still a lot of stuff to be boxed up and transported. I would need to do several trips over there in my little Renault 5 so I could take some of it with me. I was going to be playing the mind-game I refer to in *Sell the Pig*: fox, chicken, corn, river. Where you have to get a fox, a chicken and some corn across a river in a boat in two trips, without ever leaving the fox alone with the chicken, or the chicken alone with the corn.

When I first took the horses over in the big lorry we had bought, they were going to be left in the care of my friend the farrier's wife until my return. She and her husband had been posted back to the UK. She was bored and missing horses so had jumped at the chance of babysitting Blue Well and my horses for a few weeks.

I was going to have to go over with the Renault, leave it there and come back by train, then go back with the lorry and return to Germany in the Renault. I was obliged to return to Germany briefly as the editor of the paper had booked some leave and there was only me to cover it.

Once The Other Half had left for the South Atlantic, I could get to serious grips with packing the house up. One day as I was working away at boxing up all our worldly goods, there was a ring on the doorbell. I opened it to find Marty standing there.

Knowing The Other Half was away, he'd kindly come to offer his services, in case I needed a hand with anything. I had to stifle the giggles when he told me he was good at humping. I genuinely don't think he knew the double meaning of the word and meant, in all innocence, packing and shifting boxes.

There were still a lot of loose ends to be tied up on both sides of the English Channel. I would need to make several trips over there before the sale could be completed. Marty was still keen on the idea of a partnership and with that in mind, he was eager to have a look at the place.

He suggested he come with me on one trip and offered to drive, his Mazda being considerably speedier and more comfortable than the little Renault for long journeys.

My brother kindly offered us the use of his house in Wales to stay in on our visit. He had had to leave the Royal Fleet Auxiliary because of ill health and was currently working for the European Commission in Brussels. I'd been to visit him there. He was not doing terribly well as things were not good between him and his wife. She'd temporarily moved out of their home so it was standing empty and he said we were welcome to use it.

Marty and I were good friends by now. I appreciated his help and support. There was no question that we were actually going to sleep together at my brother's house. Certainly not. We were both grown-ups and both married. The house was a large one, with four bedrooms spread out over three floors. It was all very proper.

Yet somehow we did. Sleep together.

Did the earth move?

Oh, only off the Richter Scale.

Did the angels sing?

They won the Eurovision Song Contest.

And the Welsh National Eisteddfod.

So this was what it was meant to be like.

This is what I had been missing all this time.

Oh dear.

Chapter Twenty-one
Mats. Bath. Cork

When we woke the next day, we did that 'morning after' thing.

'Did that really happen …?'

'And was it …?'

Perhaps we should just check if it was a fluke …?'

'Okay, not a fluke, then.'

We were clearly going to have to talk about what happened next. This was not something either of us had planned. No doubt many readers won't believe that but it's true.

I'd never set out to have an affair with anyone. Even if I had, it would have been statistically hard to pick anyone less suitable, on paper, than Marty. He was more than twenty years older than me, a married man with four grown-up children. He was ex-Special Forces and, as I was soon to discover, those types could lie as easily as tell the truth. Possibly more easily.

It was only ever going to end in heartache, for a lot of people. But, as the old cliché goes, it was stronger than both of us.

I'd always been sceptical about phrases like 'to love someone beyond reason'. I suddenly understood exactly what it meant. I would have done anything to be with him.

If our relationship was going anywhere, clearly both our Other Halves would have to be told. But mine was away. More than eight thousand miles away. I could hardly phone him up and dump him.

When the menfolk were away on exercise, though clearly not during active conflict, we could make occasional phone calls to them from the Barracks. It was hard to have any sort of meaningful conversation because of the inevitable time-lag of the satellite phone. One would say something, there would be a pregnant pause, then both would start to speak at the same time. Both would stop, waiting for the other. And so it would go on. Certainly not suitable for a break-up conversation.

Marty and I decided that we would keep things quiet until The Other Half came back from the Falklands. It was only a short tour, he would be back in a couple of months. Then, if Marty and I still felt the same way about one another, we could decide what to do.

In the meantime, Marty helped to transport the horses across, together with a Sergeant Major from The Other Half's Regiment, someone else we'd got to know through the Saddle Club where he rode. He had a son and daughter who belonged to the Pony Club and I'd helped them get a first pony for the daughter. They were posted back to the UK so the pony was coming to live at Blue Well for the time being.

I went back to Germany to relieve the editor so he could go on his much-needed holiday. Ironically, the last headline I wrote before I put my final newspaper to bed was about the royal visit, which I had deftly avoided by being out of the country at the time.

I was itching to get back to Blue Well and finally take possession of my new home and future business. But first I had to make sure our married quarter was spick and span and ready to be handed over back to the Army. A process known as 'marching out'.

My first 'marching in' experience had been for the house in Bulford Camp and it had struck me as so silly I rather thought I'd accidentally wandered onto the set of *Monty Python's Flying Circus*.

A BQMS (Battery Quartermaster Sergeant), whose role

was to be in charge of all supplies, met me at the house looking officious, armed with a clipboard and pen which made him look even more so. Bear in mind that this was my first ever real contact with Forces' life.

We went from room to room while he read aloud from his inventory sheet each and every item I was taking possession of, at the end of which I signed the list.

Except we were dealing with Army-speak, in which everything is in reverse order.

I just about managed to keep a straight face for: 'Beds. Officers. Single. Two.' But for some reason I was consumed with the giggles about, 'Mat. Bath. Cork. One.'

I discovered, when we marched out of the first quarter in Germany, that it took a lot to explain away any deficiencies in the property list. Useless me trying to say that no, I couldn't produce the 'Curtain. Door. Front. Net. One' because Pez the German Shepherd Dog had eaten it. He'd got enraged one time that somebody had the temerity to ring the front door bell when his mistress was not at home. He'd hurled himself at the door, fortunately brand new, doubled glazed and sturdy, and torn down the curtain. He'd then ripped it into pieces and eaten some of them.

And no, I hadn't kept any of the ensuing dog poo with little bits of white nylon net in it to prove my story.

I couldn't wait to leave all of that behind me and to get back to Blue Well. I was missing the horses, for one thing. Aslan and I were particularly close and it was clear that he had been missing me, too. He and Chieftain had joined the resident Blue Well horses and were living out on the moorland surrounding the property, being brought in once a day for feeding and checking over by my friend in residence, but not doing any work.

There were two tracks from the narrow country road down to the property itself, both of them around three hundred yards long. The surrounding moorland extended to several hundred acres and had all sorts of valleys and depressions in the land where horses who didn't feel like working could hide themselves away.

The minute my little metallic champagne-coloured Renault 5 appeared at the top of that long track, it was like a *Champion the Wonder Horse* moment. In the distance I could see the small, high-speed shape of an Aslan in full flight, galloping towards my car as fast as his legs could carry him.

Thank goodness for electric windows. I could see he had no intention of stopping until he'd make physical contact with his mum. I let the window down, his head appeared through the gap and he took hold of me in his rubbery lips. He hung on to me as I drove slowly and carefully down the track to the house, with him trotting beside the car. I think he was pleased to see me.

Those early days at Blue Well were wonderful, despite the hard work and constant battles with the weather, and the quirks of the plumbing system. The kitchen alongside the barn-restaurant had a big multi-fuel range which provided hot water, cooking facilities and heated a couple of radiators. Nothing so posh as an Aga, just a humble old Tirolia, with attitude.

If we cranked it up high enough to do the cooking, the water had a tendency to get too hot and to start boiling in the tank. If no one was near enough to run some off, it would start spraying out from any weak joints in the pipework, which was hazardous to say the least.

I'd had to call in a plumber before anyone was scalded to death. He was working away on something inside the airing cupboard. I told him that a lot of the plumbing and electrics around the place seemed to have been a bit bungled. I advanced my theory that perhaps whoever had installed it all had got a DIY book out of the library and turned over two pages at once.

The plumber was a dry sort of a character. He was quiet for a long moment. Then he withdrew his lugubrious face and looked at me.

'You're wrong,' he said. 'It was four pages.'

The best part of the early days was that Marty came to stay, often. The cover story, which seemed to appease both our Other Halves, was that he was helping me get the business going and seeing whether or not his ideas for a partnership would work.

That's when I discovered what an adept liar he was. It should have been an early warning sign.

I had taken up residence in the chalet as the cottage needed a bit of work to make it comfortably habitable. Springtime in Wales is not all gambolling lambs and bursting daffodils. It can be cold, and unremittingly wet. They say, only partly in jest, that in Wales, if you can see the hills, it's going to rain. If you can't see the hills, it's raining.

When visitors came for a weekend or even longer, I would often have to spend the time describing the beautiful views to them as nothing was visible through the unrelenting murk.

The chalet, with its big, single-glazed windows, had all the insulation properties of a sieve. But it did have a Jøtul cast-iron wood burner which was marvellous. It threw out no end of heat and could be throttled right down to stay warm through the night.

There was no telephone in the chalet but I'd rigged up a long series of extension leads to put one in there, run from the main phone socket in the cottage. There was a loud outside bell so phone calls were never missed, in case it was someone wanting to book a ride or a holiday. I had enough cable to get the phone as far as the chalet's bathroom but no further, so it balanced precariously on top of the cistern above the loo.

It was impossible to have any kind of a private conversation if there was anyone else in the chalet. Marty would get out of bed from making love to me, pad into the bathroom and phone his wife. He was, he would assure her, currently staying with my brother at his house some thirty miles from Blue Well and no, he hadn't seen me nor did he have any plans to on this particular trip. He had fish of his own to fry this time. He seemed to allay any concerns she may have had about the time he and I were spending together.

He was so convincing I half believed him myself.

I'd started riding the various horses I'd acquired to assess them for customer use. I discovered that Sula's reputation was not unjust. He really did bolt. Aslan was more of a runaway. I always had some degree of control of him, after a fashion, usually a bit of steering, and I could eventually stop him if I needed to. Sula was a definite blind bolter, with all semblance of control lost.

The first time he showed his true colours we were hacking out alone, on the home moor, the one surrounding the property. I was riding Sula and leading Wags, so I could exercise both of them at once.

We were meant to be trotting. We started out that way. Then the brakes failed. Totally. His previous owners had put him in a Blair's pattern hackamore, a bitless bridle. It was proving to be as effective as throwing an empty crisp packet at a runaway train would be in stopping it.

I was used to hairy rides, thanks to Aslan. But what was concerning me was that our trajectory was taking us towards a cattle grid, and I knew Sula's history. I was also having difficulty hanging on to Wags who was no match for Sula's speed even when he wasn't in runaway mode.

Luckily, though I'm still not sure how, I managed to stop them both before the grid and we hacked carefully back home in walk, my legs more than a bit shaky after the excitement. Definitely not a safe horse to put paying customers on, unless I knew their capabilities very well.

Sometimes, with a bolter, rather than trying to stop them, it works better just to have the room to let them go until they want to stop, then make them carry on a bit longer. I decided to start training Sula up for Competitive Trail Riding, making good use of all those thousands of acres and miles of tracks inside Brechfa Forest.

Looking back, it was all a bit crazy. There were no mobile phones then so I was riding off deep into a forest on my own on a horse with no brakes. Parts of the forest were so little used that I could ride for hours without seeing a living soul. And I did ride for hours.

I was training Sula up for his first twenty-five miler so most of our serious training sessions needed to be at least four hours. If anything had happened to me, my remains would probably not have been found for ages. I would occasionally encounter Forestry Commission workers driving their vehicles through there. More than once they stopped to ask me for directions.

The first time Sula decided to bolt on those long trail rides, I simply pointed him at the nearest uphill track and let him go. It was a long old climb and when we got to the top he was slowing up, needing a breather. I kicked him on and we kept going a bit further. And a bit further.

He was a clever horse and he soon got the message. He never bolted with me again. I'd experimented with different bits for him and now had him in a simple loose-ring snaffle which certainly gave me a lot more control than the bitless bridle had.

I judged him to be ready for his first competition, which was being held locally. Marty was coming with me to act as ground crew. Even on the shorter rides, it's nice to have someone to meet you at various points on the route with a bucket of water for the horse and something cold to drink for the rider. He made an excellent second. Sula went brilliantly and passed the vettings with no trouble at all. All the training had paid off.

There was always a lot of hanging round at the end of the competitions until those on the longer trails had finished, then all the prizes could be handed out at the same time in a little formal ceremony.

I thought we'd probably done quite well but I was thrilled with our final results. Sula had won his novice class, with zero penalties, and also picked up the awards for Best Welsh Cob or Part-bred, Best Local Entry, plus a couple of others. I also got the Best Tyro Rider trophy, to my embarrassment. Technically I qualified for it since it was my first such competition in the UK under the rules of the Endurance Horse and Pony Society of Great Britain.

When we got home and had seen to Sula, making sure he was comfortable after all his efforts, although he still seemed raring to go, Marty and I went back to the chalet to stir the woodburner into life and get the kettle on for a much-needed cup of tea.

While we waited for it to boil, he put his arms rounds me and said quietly, 'I was so proud of you today, when you did so well and picked up all those prizes.'

It struck me that nobody had ever said that to me before in my life. Not my parents, never a teacher at school. Nobody.

How I loved Marty at that moment.

Chapter Twenty-two
A Diplomatic Incident

Now I was in full-time residence at Blue Well, I was anxious to start taking PGs (Paying Guests) as soon as possible, to generate a bit of income. The accommodation was still a bit basic but I'd given everywhere a thorough clean or, as my mother would call it, a good bottoming. And there was no denying that the riding was superb.

My first PGs were a nice young couple, with a strange reason for booking. She had apparently been to Blue Well when she was much younger, on one of the unaccompanied children's holidays, and had stayed in the infamous 'bunkhouse'. She remembered it had rained the whole week.

No amount of bottoming could make that old shed anything like what I would call fit for human habitation. The location wasn't very nice either, tucked away down in a dip at the side of the house. I had relegated it to the status it should always have had, that of a poultry house.

But she'd retained fond memories of the riding and the scenery so had persuaded her partner to come with her to see if things had improved since her last visit.

I'd sorted out one of the residential caravans for them and made sure they had the best horses for their level of riding. I couldn't do anything about the weather, but I could ensure that they had some wonderful rides. She voted it a brilliant holiday, much better than her previous experience. Although, of course, it still rained a lot. It was Wales, after all.

As I was still into Competitive Trail Riding, I was keen that Blue Well should host one of the prestigious hundred-mile events. It was ideally placed for the start and finish point and there was no problem at all in finding suitable routes for even the longest of the different levels of ride which would take place over the two days of the competition.

I'd been going to local committee meetings of the organisation which oversaw the competitions, to find out what was involved. Long distance riders tend to be rather obsessive types, of necessity. Think *The Loneliness of the Long Distance Runner*.

For a start riders would spend hours training, often alone, working constantly for peak fitness and performance levels. Then, because of the competition rules, there was always that worry that completing the course in the set time would not be enough because of the dreaded final vetting. Anything could happen to snatch defeat from the jaws of victory, and often did.

Someone I knew in Germany, who competed on a young Haflinger stallion, found that out to her cost. She'd finished the trail with zero penalties, had spent the two hours before the final vetting taking good care of her horse so he would present calm, supple and looking as fit as a flea.

The vetting was being held in an indoor school because of adverse weather. Just as she was going in for the examination and trot-up, someone accidentally turned on the overhead sprinklers. Her horse did a vertical take-off and his pulse went through the roof. An unsympathetic vet refused to make allowances for extenuating circumstances so they were eliminated.

The local meetings were held at the stables of my nearest rival, you could say, in the riding holiday business, although we were offering slightly different packages. It was there Sula and I had had our first successful outing together. She was a competitor herself, very dedicated, very intense.

It was just my luck that the one and only time I got Marty to go with me to one of the meetings she decided to hold forth on the subject of pulse rates. An important subject to long-distance riders, of course, as the anecdote above shows. But this was not just pulse rates in general. It was specifically the pulse rates of her own competition horse. And she seemed to talk about them for an hour or so.

Of course it probably wasn't anything like that long. But she did go on rather a bit, and I kept having to jab Marty in the ribs with an elbow to stop him falling asleep and snoring.

I've never done things by halves. As well as hosting the forthcoming ride, called the Red Dragon, I intended to compete in it on both days. A twenty-five miler on each day, Sula one day, Aslan the next. In addition, I would be accepting bookings for bed, breakfast and evening meals for officials and competitors.

When enquiries were made for rooms, I stressed to everyone that it was rudimentary, not luxury, at a price which reflected that. Usually, all the competitors were interested in was something to eat and somewhere dry and not too cold to lay their weary heads. Even better if there was the chance to rent a field or stable for their horse for a night or two. Sometimes the horses slept on the lorry they had come in and there was enough parking to allow for that.

All of these people were going to want feeding, of course, so I would need reinforcements to help with that. We would be offering breakfast, afternoon tea and scones, and supper for anyone who wanted it.

My brother's wife jumped at the chance of helping. She and my brother were gradually drifting further apart but she adored horses and anything to do with them, so she loved spending time with me at Blue Well. She was also a good cook and not afraid of hard work. In addition, the wife of the Sergeant Major who had his daughter's pony at livery was also a cook, and a grafter. The two of them, both large and formidable ladies, would be in charge of the kitchen and of feeding the ravening hordes.

One of the officiating vets was going to be staying on site and had booked accommodation for himself, his wife and two children. As I was a married woman living with someone else's husband, I was not on the moral high ground to judge anyone. It still amused me that, when someone was asking for the vet and I in turn asked one of the children where her father was, she drew herself up to her full height, gave me a withering look and retorted, 'That isn't Daddy. That's Mummy's friend.'

The family also annoyingly turned up with a small dog, without having asked if it would be acceptable. As it turned out, it wasn't. They didn't supervise it at all, so that, as I was opening the door to one of the bedrooms to show people their accommodation for the night, I saw that the dog had been in the room and left his calling card, in the shape of a pile of dog poo, on one of the beds. So as if I didn't have enough to do, I had to strip the bed, wash everything, and find clean linen to put on it.

Inevitably, because we were full to capacity and all running round like headless chickens, the kitchen range decided to be at its least cooperative. It would either barely go at all, with about as much heat output as a candle, or it would roar away like a blast furnace. This caused the hot water cylinder to boil over, making groaning noises and causing the pipes to gurgle and whistle alarmingly.

I was mostly on yard duties in the morning as all of my horses needed feeding and mucking out, not just the ones I was competing on. Once that was done, I went into the kitchen to get some much-needed tea and to see if the cooks, Debs and Jackie, had everything under control.

Just at that moment, the same child I had spoken to the day before came in, looking even more imperious than ever. She said Mummy had sent her to ask if she could have her breakfast in bed.

Apart from the fact that we were clearly run ragged, what we were charging for accommodation barely covered the laundry bills and food, never mind room service.

I was trying to formulate a tactful response but Debs beat me to it. She was tall and imposing, well-spoken, from a posh part of Surrey. But she had a mouth like a fishwife when crossed. Barely pausing in flipping the bacon and frying the eggs, she threw over her shoulder, 'No, she can't. Tell her to f*ck orf.'

The child turned obediently and started to go on her way. Not wanting a diplomatic incident before the competition had even started, I raced after her to explain that what the lady meant to say was that we were really rather busy. Perhaps she would ask Mummy if she could possibly manage to come over to the dining room – like everyone else was doing.

With the amount of hard work that went into the hosting the event, we decided collectively that it wasn't something we would rush to repeat. It had been a good PR exercise, though. A lot of people had seen that Blue Well was once more very much up and running. Especially that the horses there were competing and doing well.

I decided that it might be fun, in the future, to host a couple of the smaller events and encourage our growing set of regular local riders to compete in them. Because as well as setting up the residential holiday side of the business, I was getting locals who wanted good riding, on decent horses, booking to go out for hacks with me. It was how I was to meet one of my best friends ever.

Debs, my sister-in-law, came to help me whenever she could, loving the excuse to change out of her hospital sister's uniform, don her wellies and play with horses. We'd also acquired a young local man, Simon, who'd offered to come and do some odd jobs in exchange for learning to ride. He was planning to join the Army and had time on his hands before he went.

Afternoon tea was always a big thing at Blue Well. We would offer it, at a modest fee, for customers, especially at the end of one of the long day-rides I was now taking out, having discovered some wonderful five-hour rides with hardly any roadwork.

Once we were back and the horses had been seen to then turned back out onto the moor to have a good roll and a graze, everyone would adjourn to the barn dining room for tea and cakes or scones.

Debs and I were both adept at knocking up tasty cakes, and we'd taught young Simon how to make more than presentable scones. On this particular occasion, the delicacy on offer was a Victoria sandwich cake and, as we weren't expecting many punters, there was only one piece left. Knowing what a gannet Simon could be, I very pointedly picked it up and licked it before riding out, so I could be sure it would still be waiting for me when I returned.

The rider I was taking out was a woman called Jill, a lecturer in Agricultural Sciences at a local college. We were destined to become good friends, despite me having to explain to her, when we got back from the ride and I invited her in for a cup of tea, the reason why I couldn't offer her any of the delicious cake sitting in the middle of the table.

But things were about to get a bit complicated. The Other Half was due back from the Falklands any time now, and as soon as he got back he would be coming over to Blue Well, no doubt expecting a romantic reunion.

Marty, wisely, made himself scarce. He was still in the UK but wasn't going to hang around when The Other Half came home. We needed to coordinate each telling our Other Half at the same time, to prevent either finding out first. I was still convinced we were madly in love and that my future now lay with him. He took himself off to visit some of his four children.

It was not going to be easy. I couldn't suddenly magic up

feelings for The Other Half which I no longer had. At the same time, I didn't want to hurt him, as none of this was really his fault. But if I'd ever thought myself in love with him, I now knew that I wasn't, and didn't really want to be with him.

The when and the how of broaching the subject with him were taken out of my hands in an unexpected way. We'd survived a few days and awkward nights of me being tired or having a headache. Then one evening, the phone on top of the toilet cistern in the chalet rang.

It was Marty's wife, Pat, demanding to speak to The Other Half.

It caught me completely by surprise. I didn't know she knew. But just from her tone, she clearly did. I hung up.

She rang straight back. She was insistent. She could either speak to him now or wait until he got back to Germany and speak to him then.

It wasn't at all how I'd planned it to come out. But perhaps it was a way of forcing the issue. I called him to the phone.

Afterwards, The Other Half and I spoke for a long time. I despise clichés in writing, but I probably used most of them in talking to him.

'It's not you, it's me ...'

'We never planned any of this ...'

'We never meant to hurt either of you ...'

And so on.

For some bizarre reason, The Other Half insisted that he wanted to see Marty, face-to-face, to tell him exactly what he thought of him. I wasn't worried that it would get violent. It seemed pointless to me, but I felt that if that's what he wanted, it was only reasonable to agree.

I could never contact Marty, not throughout any of our time together. There were no mobile phones back then and he was always evasive about where he was going. It should have been a warning sign. He'd arranged to phone me soon after The Other Half's return. When he did, I told him what had happened and, to his credit, he agreed to come as soon as he could.

The encounter seemed to me to be bordering on the farcical. The Other Half insisted on telling Marty he was a cad. I thought that only happened in Victorian melodrama. But it appeared to make him feel better, and Marty sat and took it with good grace.

Then we had something of a civilised conversation to decide how we were all going to go forward. There was no mention of divorce. It was not what any of us was looking for. I certainly had no intention of ever remarrying.

It was agreed that The Other Half would continue to pay the mortgage on Blue Well and was free to visit whenever he chose, when Marty would absent himself. Marty could stay, as long as he worked for his keep, helped to run the business and made himself scarce whenever necessary.

I would continue to run the business, without taking a wage. To work hard to make sure I generated enough income to cover all costs.

It seemed, for the time being, as if we might have a workable solution.

Chapter Twenty-three
Gale Force

Now that The Other Halves knew, it only remained for me to tell my parents. Marty had none to worry about.

Unsurprisingly, my religious father, Holy Joe, was disapproving. It didn't bother me in the slightest. We'd never been particularly close and had grown even less so of late. His opinion was of neither interest nor significance to me.

My mother came for a visit, at a time when Marty was in residence. I carefully explained to her my new domestic arrangements. She was very upset. She could barely bring herself to speak to Marty, although he was polite and courteous to her. She spent a lot of time in floods of tears saying she wanted to go home.

I was disappointed. I didn't know a lot about normal family life. Our home life was far from it. My father had always spent much of his time belittling my brother and only showing an interest in either of us when there were visitors around. I remained convinced that his actions were in no small part to blame for my brother's later serious mental health issues, especially his bouts of depression and his low self-esteem.

But I thought mothers were supposed to be different. I thought they were meant to support their children in their craziest of decisions, as long as it made them happy. And I was happy with Marty. You only needed to spend a few minutes in our company when we were together to realise that. Certainly much happier than I had ever been as an Army wife, with The Other Half.

My mother, however, couldn't cope. Her way of dealing with it was to ignore the situation. From then on, she only ever visited when Marty was away. If I visited her, she would force herself to ask after him, but it was always through tightly gritted teeth.

My sister-in-law, Debs, knew the situation, of course, as did my brother. Marty and I had called on him once in Brussels on our travels. The two of them appeared to get on quite well together.

Marty was determined to pay his own way at Blue Well. He wanted a source of income so nobody could add accusations of living off either me or The Other Half to his list of perceived crimes. I knew he was a yachtsman with a skipper's licence. He told me he'd sailed with Chay Blyth. I never knew which of his tales was true but it was possible, since they had both been in the Parachute Regiment.

He said he could make some reasonable money getting work delivering boats from Britain down to the Med and other places. It would mean him going away, sometimes for a few weeks at a time, when he would be out of contact.

By now I was gearing up for the main part of the holiday season, which was going to be unaccompanied children's riding holidays. I knew it was going to be a lot of work and long hours. It meant not even having enough time to miss him all that much.

There were more horses and ponies now, so I could take more customers at a time. Some were on loan, including some of the bigger ones. People who hunted were sometimes happy to lend their horses out through the summer so they could be worked enough to be fit and ready for the coming season. I also had three small ponies which doting grandparents had bought for their grandchildren, who were coming to me for lessons.

Those three ponies, Flossie, Cindy and Blackie belonged to

people in the next village who were going to become my surrogate parents. Their names were Cole and Sylve and they were some of the nicest, warmest-hearted people I'd ever met. If ever I was on my own or in need, there was always a meal and a warm welcome for me at their home.

Sylve had always wanted to learn to ride but had always been afraid. I persuaded her to let me teach her. I'd made a study of teaching nervous riders because I could empathise with their fear. I'd only learnt to swim as an adult, by having private lessons with someone who understood my terror, born out of bullying teachers and outdated methods used on me as a child.

The first time Sylve came for a lesson, I chose steady old Barney for her. He would stand patiently and rock-still next to the mounting block and wait for as long as it took for his rider to climb aboard.

We must have spent half that first session just getting Sylve into the saddle, and we only walked the length of the yard and back. But after taking that first huge leap of faith, she graduated to riding Chieftain and coming out with me on slow, steady hacks in the forest. She had no ambition ever to do more than a gentle jog, but how she loved those rides.

The idea behind the children's residential holidays was that the visitors could get the experience of 'owning' their own pony for a week. They were matched with a suitable one and they were responsible for taking care of it, under supervision.

I didn't want it to be like boarding school, but a few rules were essential. I did a morning room inspection after which the children had time to prepare themselves and their ponies for the day's rides. Marks were awarded for good turnout and at the end of the week, there was a prize for the one who had looked after their pony best.

There was no official lights out time at night, but one rule was sacrosanct and heaven help anyone who broke it. My bedroom adjoined the annexe where the children slept, and with all the work and responsibility, I needed my sleep. If ever they made so much noise, after ten o'clock at night, that I had to get out of my bed to go round there to tell them to be quiet, the riding activity for the following day would be cancelled. It was a way of teaching respect for others. I only had to enforce the rule once in all the years I ran the holidays.

In theory, I was accepting unaccompanied children between ten and sixteen years old. I would occasionally drop the age. My youngest ever came with her family when she was just five. I'm still good friends with her parents. We've stayed in touch with one another ever since and visited each other in our new homes.

Sometimes the children would travel independently, getting a train or coach from various parts of the country which would take them to Carmarthen, where I would meet them.

The first time I went to collect some of them from the bus station, I was astounded at how grown up the children looked. When I'd been a horse-mad twelve-year-old, I practically lived in my jodhpurs all the time. I would almost certainly have travelled in them to go on a horsey holiday.

I'd had Blue Well Riding Centre sweatshirts made, which children could buy as a souvenir of their holiday, and I always wore one when going to pick them up from the coach or the train. On the coaches, in those days, the driver would keep an eye on children travelling alone and make sure they were handed over to an appropriate adult. My 'uniform' made me easy to spot.

I was looking for small, eager, horsey girls. The two who approached me were both taller than me, wearing make-up, dressed to kill and looking about eighteen. I was worried about what they would make of Blue Well and its basic accommodation.

Luckily, the moment any of them met the pony which was to be 'theirs' for the week, it was always love at first sight. Even these two glamour girls, within a day, were muddy, bedraggled, covered in hay and horsehair and clearly having the time of their lives.

Saturday was our changeover day. New arrivals came in the afternoon and departed the following Saturday morning. The horses had the day off work and often didn't even bother to come in for food most weeks. They quickly learned the routine.

For us humans, the day was a flurry of activity. The minute one lot of guests had departed, we had to strip and remake all the beds, do the laundry, clean everything in sight and make sure everywhere looked spick-and-span.

Debs and Simon were always on hand to help me. As we got busier, I started to take overseas students who would come and work for their keep and a chance to improve their English. If we all worked really hard together, we could sometimes manage to finish in time to collapse in a heap, hopefully in the sunshine if it wasn't raining, for an hour or two, before the incoming arrivals.

The children's weeks were packed with activities. The fun started with a scavenger hunt, where they worked in twos and were given a list of things they had to collect. A white stone, a nettle, a twig, a feather, and so on. There was always a tie-breaker, in case they all managed to find everything. Sometimes it would be something easy, like the roundest pebble. Other times, for older children, it would be a bit of a brain-teaser, like a picture of the Queen.

There were day rides, with picnic lunches, gymkhana games and jumping competitions, a mock hunt, like a mounted version of Hare and Hounds. But the highlight of the week was always playing Cowboys and Indians.

Health and Safety regulations these days would have prevented any such thing, but it was always fun and safe. There were two teams, Cowboys and Indians, who would go out separately and track one another through the forest, with a pitched battle when they met. Each team would have a token, a standard. Sometimes just a headscarf on a stick. The winning team was the one could take the standard from the others.

On the evening of Cowboys and Indians day, as long as the weather allowed, we always had a bonfire and barbecue, plus mock scalping of the losing team.

To enter into the spirit of it, the Indians always wore war paint, and painted up their ponies. I always led the Indian team, face painted, wearing a costume as befitted an Indian chief. It became so commonplace I tended to forget I was dressed like that.

As well as the residential side of the business, I also gave private riding lessons and took people out hacking. One day someone came to enquire about dressage lessons. I told them what I could offer, saying that I competed in dressage and one-day eventing on several of the school horses, so could find one of the required standard for them.

The person looked unconvinced. They asked about my BHS qualifications. It took longer than it should have for the penny to drop. They were clearly having difficulty with the concept of taking dressage lessons from a war-painted Indian chief.

When Marty was there, he pitched in and helped with anything and everything. Because we lived next to such a huge forest, there was no shortage of timber for the fires in the chalet and in the cottage. I'd found time to clean that up a bit and was now living in it, so the chalet could be used for paying guests, providing more revenue.

The forest was maintained by the Forestry Commission and anyone living nearby could buy a permit to forage for fallen wood for burning. You weren't allowed to cut anything down or to take anything which had been logged, but you could have all the fallen branches and timber you could transport for a nominal sum.

We still had the four-horse lorry in which Aslan, Chieftain and Pascha the pony travelled back from Germany. That meant lots of room for firewood. Whenever we had a quiet moment, which was admittedly not often, Marty and I would go into the woods and collect as much as we could gather and load. Being resinous, it burnt well and certainly helped us keep the place a bit warmer.

I'm not about to claim any mystic powers or to say I have second sight or anything. But sometimes, when you are very close to someone, you seem to know things about them even when you're not in direct contact. I'm sure most of us have experienced that strange thing where you decide to phone your best friend or a family member. Then when you get up to do so, the phone rings and it's them calling you.

I felt especially close to Marty. Closer than I'd ever felt to The Other Half. I was not naive enough to imagine I was his first fling. Early on in our affair, just after his wife found out, she would phone me up to rant at me. I wasn't his first, she told me, and doubtless wouldn't be his last. I didn't really care. It was all about living in the moment, as far as I was concerned. And the moments, when he was there with me, especially when there were no PGs or anyone else to disturb us, were wonderful. Sadly, they were never long-lived.

When Marty was away at sea, it was always a worrying time as I had no means of contacting him. Sometimes, watching the television news at the end of a long day's work, I'd see reports of horrendous weather conditions in areas where I knew he could well be sailing. It was always nerve-wracking when there was no news of him within the time-frame he'd given me for his likely return.

On one such occasion the news footage of the seas off the British coast was terrifying. There was still no word from Marty. Debs and Simon could see my anxiety and were trying to make reassuring noises. He was an experienced sailor, he'd sailed several oceans, he could cope with weather like that, including rounding Cape Horn.

Then the next morning, when we all met up in the big

kitchen for breakfast, I was smiling, relaxed, happy again. They were both surprised, wondering what I had to smile about. They asked if Marty had phoned, although both of them would have heard the outside bell if he had.

I told them confidently that Marty was fine. He was safely anchored in Cornwall and all was well. They both looked at me strangely. He wasn't meant to be docking in Cornwall; it wasn't on his planned route.

Just as we were starting our breakfast, the shrill outside bell on the side of the cottage rang. Beaming, I jumped up from the table and rushed across to the house to answer it.

Marty. Safely ashore from bad storms, gusting to gale force. Now harboured in Cornwall.

Chapter Twenty-four
Return to Sender

Marty's stays with me were getting fewer and further between. There was always a seemingly plausible explanation for his absence, apart from the sailing trips to earn some money. One time it was that his young daughter was ill. Another time that his wife was.

I had vowed never to play the jealous lover card, having a tantrum every time he returned to see his family. I knew it was the kiss of death in so many relationships. I firmly believed that you had to let someone go in order for them to come back to you. So far, it had worked.

We had a bit of a scare early on, not long after The Other Halves had found out about us. Marty was still trying to be honourable, staying in touch with his wife to make sure she was doing as well as she could in the circumstances. He was also, of course, anxious to hear about his dog.

One day he'd been trying for hours to phone her, with no reply. He told me this; he didn't hide from me the fact that he stayed in touch. With my strange witchy-woo second sight, I immediately told him that he couldn't get hold of her because she was behind the wheel of her car heading in our direction like an avenging fury. He told me she would never do something like that. He sounded as if he was trying to convince himself of that.

We spent an anxious night, Marty because he was clearly

worried what had happened to his wife, worried that she might have done something stupid. I was concerned that at any minute she might turn up on the doorstep unannounced.

She so nearly did. We got a phone call quite early the following morning. Marty leapt for the phone in case it was news of Pat. It was. She had driven non-stop through the night, except for the short ferry crossing over the Channel, which had caused the car to boil over. She was now stranded at the side of the M4 motorway.

She'd so nearly turned up unannounced. If she'd not been in such a hurry that she forgot to check the coolant level in her car, she would have arrived and probably found us in bed together. Goodness knows what might have happened then.

Marty didn't have his precious Mazda with him. He never brought it to Blue Well. The track would have been catastrophic for its low undercarriage. Which meant that he was not independently mobile. I still had my Renault 5. He asked me if he could possibly borrow my car to go and rescue his wife.

If they gave out rosettes for 'Most understanding mistress', I think I would have swept the board in all classes. Without a murmur I handed over the keys, told him to take care and said I hoped he could sort things out and point Pat back in the direction from which she had come.

Goodness knows what possessed him, but a few hours later Marty turned up back at Blue Well with Pat in the passenger seat of my car. I'd rather thought he'd fix the car and send her on her way. But no. Here she was, on my home ground, looking at me as if she would quite like to kill me.

It was perhaps fortuitous that I had been out on the moorland, fixing some of the perimeter fencing from the outside. And I was armed with an eleven-pound log maul which I'd been using as a post driver. If you're not familiar with one, it's like an obese axe head, a thick wedge shape of heavy metal. Handled skilfully, and I wasn't bad with it, it could split quite a big log in half. It could certainly do some considerable damage to a person if they got too close to it.

Seeing me coming back down the track with the maul slung over my shoulder, Marty very wisely ordered his wife to remain in the car. My car. He told me she'd wanted to see the place, to see if she could understand why it – and I – seemed to have him under our spell. But now she'd seen it, if I would kindly let him use my car for a bit longer, he would drive her back to hers, get it fixed and send her straight back to Germany.

He came back to me. He always came back. Eventually. He was still proclaiming his love for me and talking about us finally being together, one day. He told me that there was still family property back in Zimbabwe and that he would be coming into some money for it. He suggested we could use that to get a place together, rather than living somewhere which I jointly owned with The Other Half. It all sounded wonderful.

When I was with him, I believed in the dream. When I wasn't, I took the view that I would believe it when I saw it. I was still in love with him – dangerously so – but I was not so deluded as to believe everything he told me. Not with his background.

My brother was intrigued by the mysterious enigma which was Marty. He was convinced that there was more to him than met the eye. He even suggested that his absences were linked to something at best covert, at worst criminal. Something like arms dealing.

It was true that one of his trips had coincided with us seeing something on TV about a shipment of arms being seized somewhere in the Channel, but details were scarce in those days before the internet. And my brother was something of a Walter Mitty who loved to tell a good story and wasn't averse to embellishing it a bit.

One of the ships he served on in his Royal Fleet Auxiliary days was the support vessel for the minesweeper HMS

Bronington while it was under the command of Prince Charles, the Prince of Wales.

The story of his life, my brother was once more taken ill whilst on board. All his life, he had reacted to any sort of stress by being ill. Sometimes spectacularly so, with much projectile vomiting. It may well have been psychosomatic but the symptoms were always realistic. With his medical training, he could conjure up all sorts of things for his imagination to inflict on his body.

On this occasion, whoever saw to him, as he was often the acting Medical Officer on board, decided there was a distinct possibility that he had appendicitis. Since they were in the Med, the preferred option was to airlift him by helicopter to the Royal Naval Hospital in Gibraltar, the nearest port with suitable facilities.

I hate flying and wouldn't get into a helicopter at gunpoint. My brother was ten times worse. He became hysterical at the mere suggestion. The only thing to be done was for his vessel, which was, I think, called the Grey Rover, to go full steam ahead and head for shore.

Grey Rover had a top speed of nineteen knots. Prince Charles' ship, Bronington, could only manage thirteen. So the manoeuvre involved leaving the heir to the throne chugging along behind unattended trying to keep his escort vehicle in sight.

In those pre-email days everything was done by old-fashioned letters. The one my brother sent me describing the incident was a classic and I so wished it had not been lost in the various house moves I've made. It included a wonderful cartoon of an irate Prince jumping up and down on the bridge, shaking a first and shouting, 'Wait for me!' at Grey Rover's retreating wake.

Bearing this propensity of his in mind, I was never sure about my brother's tale of trying to dig into Marty's background. My brother was still working in Brussels at the time and hinted that his role included some interesting work which brought him into contact with people who knew people. He took advantage of this to ask a few questions about Marty.

I'll never know now what the truth of the tale was but my brother swore blind that shortly after setting the ball rolling, two men in suits came to his flat in Etterbeek and told him to stop asking questions. Who knows what really happened. But something certainly rattled my brother as, unusually for him, he didn't want to talk about it much.

Whatever the true reason behind Marty's absences, it made for some intense reunions. It must be true that absence makes the heart grow fonder as there was no sign of our mutual attraction cooling off. To put it bluntly, we could never wait to rip the clothes off one another.

On one memorable occasion, we were supposed to be doing some job or another in the back garden. Suffice it to say that not a lot of DIY got done and we were both relieved that there were no walkers out on the moor which adjoined the property on three sides and overlooked the strip of grass we rather grandly called a lawn.

Such moments of intense passion were bound to make pulses race. Marty became a bit neurotic about his, however. He talked of needing to see a cardiologist – more absences.

When he came back from his consultation, he told me that he'd been told he needed to have a pacemaker fitted. He was booked into a London hospital for the simple procedure. I offered to go and visit him while he was there. I was sure Debs or someone would mind the shop for me while I was gone. He declined, saying he wouldn't be in for long enough to make it worthwhile.

I'd long since discovered there was no point pushing him. He could make a mule appear reasonable. If I tried to insist on anything, the shutters came down with a clang.

I decided to try a compromise. I strongly suspected that the reason he was shutting me out was that his wife and perhaps some of his children might visit him in hospital and he didn't want any confrontational scenes if I happened to turn up at the same time as any of them.

If I wasn't allowed to visit him, I asked him if I could at least send him a card, just to show I was thinking of him. I persuaded him to give me the hospital address, with the ward he would be on.

I wasn't deliberately trying to catch him out. But it occurred to me often that I really had no idea where he was most of the time. I only ever had his word for it.

I chose a nice card for him, not too soppy, and sent it off. I was in the habit of always putting a return address on the back of any envelope I sent and I did the same this time, not thinking twice about it.

My card bounced back faster than a high-speed boomerang. 'Return to sender,' was written in an officious hand. 'No such person at this address.'

There was just a chance that it had been intercepted by his wife at his bedside as he was recovering from his operation. It looked more likely that some clerical type in the hospital had redirected it when not having found any such person listed as an in-patient.

Not long afterwards, Marty himself phoned me to say that the operation had been a success and he hoped to be 'home' at Blue Well before much longer. Mostly out of mischief, I asked him if he'd received the card I sent him and if he'd liked it.

Rather too quickly, he said he had received it and loved it, but that he had to ring off as someone was waiting to use the phone. It was the first time I had caught him out in a blatant lie.

True to his word, he did come back to Blue Well before too much longer. He was sporting a small surgical dressing just under his left collarbone, which is where a pacemaker would be inserted, if that part of his story was even true. It was just above the springbok which was tattooed on the left side of his chest.

He kept it covered whenever we were together. He didn't want me to touch it. I was intrigued as to whether or not the pacemaker could be felt through the skin. He said it was still tender to the touch so he preferred me not to prod it.

The trips away were still happening. The time we spent together was getting rarer. I still had no certain idea of where he went and what he got up to. Part of me thought it better not to know. I just clung on to the time we did spend together, which was always good.

When he turned up after one particularly protracted absence, he seemed different. Bitter, somehow. He kept telling me I was better off without him. I was still sure I wasn't.

One day when he was away a man phoned and asked to speak to Marty, by name. I was always under strict instructions to deny all knowledge of him and to say he certainly didn't live at Blue Well. Because I was never certain of exactly what he got up to and how much of it, if any, might still be work for the special forces, I did as he asked me. They do say that such special operatives never really retire. It hadn't ever arisen before this one occasion.

Sometimes in the past Marty had asked me to type something out for him, purporting to be confirmation of his entry having been accepted for a long distance ride at Blue Well on a certain date. He was clearly alibiing himself but I decided I might well be better off not knowing what it was all about.

I told the caller that he was mistaken, that there was no Marty at the number he had called. He was most insistent, saying he urgently wanted to make contact with him. Could I give him a message when next I saw him? I was equally as insistent that he had the wrong number.

When I told Marty about it he practically interrogated me, wanting to know everything the caller said and how he said it. Did he give any other details? Did he have an accent? What did he sound like? What did I say to him? What did he say to me, in detail? Was there anything else at all I could remember?

The incident had clearly rattled him.

He came and went another couple of times.

Then he went.

This time, he never came back.

Chapter Twenty-five
Business as usual

Marty had said nothing. His parting was no different from any of the others. He never had much gear with him, always living out of his kitbag. I'd never been bothered by it. Lots of ex-military were like that, finding it hard to put down roots in one place when they left the service.

There'd been the usual hugs and kisses, protestations of undying love, promises to get back as soon as he could and that next time it would be for good. We'd finally be together for the rest of our days, in a place of our own.

Yet somehow – witchy-woo? intuition? - this time, I knew it was the end.

When there's no break-up, no good-byes, it's hard to go through the feelings almost like mourning that can follow the end of an intense relationship. I was functioning, barely, on autopilot for some weeks after he left.

Thank goodness for animals. There were now some twenty horses to be looked after and I was often on my own to do it, at times when the holiday season was over and there were no PGs. Jaffa was back from her six-month incarceration in quarantine kennels. She'd been as pleased to see me as I was to get her back when she arrived.

Dogs in quarantine are not allowed to be taken out of their kennel and run for any reason, so no nice long walkies. The kennel owner had kept a careful eye on Jaffa's diet as, like a lot of spayed bitches, she had a tendency to put on weight. She arrived looking fabulous, slim, newly shampooed and blow-dried, all fluffy and sweet smelling.

I'd also got myself a second dog, a young, long-haired German Shepherd. Jaffa was a super dog, very easy, but I was missing the size and substance of Pez and hankering for another big dog. I didn't want to go to a breeder when there are always so many unwanted puppies after Christmas. So I put an advert up in the market hall in Carmarthen: 'Unwanted German Shepherd Christmas puppy very much wanted by me. Good home.'

I got a phone call from someone who did a bit of breeding and who said they had a young pup, four months old who had been born partially sighted and with a long coat, frowned upon for showing in those days. They sounded like nice people. They said they should really have put him to sleep but he was such a lively and lovable pup that they couldn't bring themselves to.

Who says coincidences don't happen in real life? How many have we had so far, just in this book? It turned out that the breeders were the same people from whom my lodger from Esgair days, Ann, who had also worked at Blue Well, had bought her GSD pup, Jingle.

I went to see them. They were a long way from being a puppy farm. Small scale, just a couple of breeding bitches, housed in nice clean runs inside a converted garage. They had both the mother and the father of the pup I had come to view and showed both to me first. Friendly, happy dogs, good temperaments, always so important with big dogs like GSDs. The eye defect had come as a complete surprise to them, but it wasn't a significant factor to me. As long as the pup could lead a full and happy life, partially-sighted, that was all I cared about.

After I'd seen the parents, they opened another run and a small and very hairy bundle of kinetic energy exploded out of it, headed straight for me, pinged up off the floor as if it were a springboard and landed on my chest. Two huge hairy paws went round my neck and a big, pink tongue, like a yard of bacon, started covering my face in soppy kisses.

The centre of his eyes was slightly cloudy and there was nystagmus - rapid eye movement – but despite that, the look appeared to be adoring and quizzical, as if he was asking, 'Are you going to be my new mummy?'

I was clearly not leaving without him, especially as those great fluffy feet were now clinging to my neck like a limpet. His pet name, the breeders told me, was Shamrock. I didn't like it. It was a bit soppy for such a big lump. But he seemed to vaguely recognise the sound of it so I changed it to Sjambok. He was to prove himself to be a valuable part of the healing process after Marty's disappearance. Always available for a lick and a cuddle on demand.

He also proved himself to be something of a natural clown. If I was trying to enjoy a quiet moment in the evening, when all the work had been done, he would inevitably be up to mischief, making noise and distracting me from trying to watch the news.

Even attempting to tell him to be quiet was pointless. He would immediately bound across the room, hurdle over the back of the sofa on which I was sitting, straight onto the top of my head. He would then amuse himself by attempting to remove my nose with his needle-sharp puppy teeth. It's impossible to maintain any shred of dignity with a large, hairy GSD sitting on your head.

Although Marty had gone, I was never on my own for long. Blue Well seemed to have a knack of attracting the right sort of people to come and stay. I'd acquired over-wintering hippies who lived in a beautifully converted coach in a corner of the land.

He, Nikolai, of Russian extraction, was something of a celebrity in hippy circles. A veteran of the infamous Battle of the Beanfield in 1985, when Wiltshire Police had clashed violently with the so-called Peace Convoy of New Age Travellers trying to set up a free festival at Stonehenge. He lived with his partner, Gay and in exchange for safe parking on my land, they did odd jobs about the place. Nik sawed firewood, Gayzie helped with the cleaning.

They happened to mention that they had a friend who was looking for somewhere to stay for a short time to get his act together. Said friend, Alex, had been living in Wales' Tipi Valley, which had gained some notoriety when it appeared on television. It was a commune of hippies, living in tipis on their own land, moving their lodges around frequently enough not to fall foul of planning regulations. A real cat and mouse game with the planning authorities.

I told them that anyone was welcome at Blue Well, as long as they weren't free-loaders. Provided that this character Alex helped around the place he could live in one of the mobile homes, as it was outside the PG season, and I'd feed him. I suggested they get him to come and see me first to see if we would be suited.

I wasn't quite sure what I was expecting. But I will never forget my first sight of Alex, striding down my driveway to meet me.

He was tall and slim, wearing a multi-coloured mohair jumper above old cords, with a battered black felt hat on his head. He had a full-face beard and long hair in a ponytail. Quintessential hippy. He had a singular way of walking, seeming to rise up and down with each long stride he took.

I liked him as soon as I saw him. He quickly became, and still is, one of my best friends. Certainly my best male friend. So let's immediately address the issue which many people always wonder about yet few dare to ask. No, we never did. Not once. It never entered our minds. It's probably the reason we have stayed such good friends for thirty years now.

Looking like he did, he should have scared away the

customers, especially the parents depositing their unaccompanied children with us for holidays. But when he greeted them with pots of tea and warm-from-the-oven scones, which he too quickly became adept at baking, and sat down to talk politely and intelligently to them, all inhibitions were instantly broken down, reservations set aside.

He freely admitted to knowing nothing about horses. He had worked as a dairy herdsman, looking after more than a hundred milking cows. He had a cattleman's contempt for horses, seeing them only as rivals for his cows' grass.

But he undoubtedly had a way with animals. My dogs loved him on sight, which was always a good sign. The most incredible thing was the way a horse called Pearl took to him.

Pearl belonged to my friend Jill, who had been riding with me since the early days and had decided to get her own horse to keep at working livery with me.

I was determined to have my own source of income, separate from the business, so I was not living off The Other Half. To that end, I did a bit of buying, selling and breeding for sale. I'd met a local man, an ex-show jumper, who did a bit of dealing. He'd suggested I went and took a look at Pearl as a possible for Jill.

She was not a big mare, 15.2hh and on the slightly built side, but as tough and as wiry as a mustang. She also had a foul temper and could take against people at the drop of a hat. Her character earned her the nickname of The Old Witch. She'd been a hunt horse, down in the Welsh Valleys. She suited Jill down to the ground, gave her many good years of rides and presented her with a huge cream-coloured colt foal, Cinnabar, who she kept for the whole of his life.

Pearl was particularly wary of men. When I went to see her, she lunged over the top of her stable door at the dealer, teeth bared, with clear murderous intent. But she was a great ride and a good jumper. Jill went to see her and try her, liked her and bought her.

Amazingly, the self-confessed horse novice Alex could do almost anything with her. He always claimed it was the all-pervading smell of weed which inevitably clung to him and which acted as a tranquilliser. Whatever his secret, it meant I could safely leave him to look after all of the horses, including The Old Witch, if ever I needed to go anywhere.

I like nicknames. It's a thing I do. Alex quickly became Alexander Beetle, after the A A Milne poem and the song by Melanie Safka, later just Beetle. He didn't stay long on the mountain that first time, but he was a good friend, one I was glad to have with me when tragedy befell us.

When you keep animals of any kind, mishaps, drama and terrible things are never far away. We were about to experience our worst to date.

Debs, my sister-in-law, had now left my brother and was living in a flat in Carmarthen with a gentleman friend. She still liked to come to Blue Well as often as possible, for the horse contact. It could have been awkward for me, caught between her and my brother. To his credit, my brother didn't begrudge her the horse time. In fact he asked me to take care of her after they split up.

She'd recently bought herself a young thoroughbred horse, Merlin. I was breaking him in for her. I'd just backed him for the first time and it had gone well. We were both excited about his future.

I'd acquired another hippy couple, John and Sarah, who were living in the chalet and helping out in lieu of paying rent. Nik and Gayzie had moved on. Sarah was horsey so was a useful helper about the place and had been a steadying influence holding Merlin the first time I'd swung a leg across his back and settled in the saddle.

Once I'd finished with him for the day, I brushed him off and turned him out to roll and relax on the back lawn with an Arab, Khassan, I'd recently bought. Then Alex and I went off to pick up a young mare who was coming in for schooling.

Quite a hot-headed chestnut mare, deserving of the reputation they can have.

A moment's inattention. A barrier which had come down and not been noticed. Merlin and Khassan coming ambling round the corner to see who the newcomer was. A squeal and a stamp from the mare. And one of Merlin's front legs shattered like fragile glass.

It was so wrong. So unfair. It hadn't even been a proper kick. It should have done no more than inflict a flesh wound. But here was this beautiful young horse, damaged beyond repair.

Which meant that instead of phoning Debs to report a successful first ride, I would have to inform her that her horse had had to be shot. Because there was no doubt about it. An injury like that simply could not be repaired.

All that could be done was for Alex to hold and comfort Merlin while I ran to phone the vet. It was the duty vet, not my regular one. I asked him to come immediately and bring a gun. Mercifully, a horse's metabolism is programmed to work in a near-miraculous way. As a prey animal, they are effectively dead from the minute they suffer a crippling injury and they know it. It's just a matter of time before they are taken by the nearest predator. So their system is immediately flooded with endorphins, which act like morphine, reducing the perception of pain. I have seen critically injured horses happily grazing and seemingly unaware of their fate.

News like that couldn't possibly be delivered over the phone. If Alex had not driven, I doubt I could have got to Debs flat. As it was, I had great difficulty telling her what had happened. Fortunately, although I'd not particularly taken to the new man in her life, he was marvellous. He said all the right things to both of us, produced tea, sent me off for a bath as I was still covered in Merlin's blood.

Picking yourself up off the floor after something like that isn't easy. But hugs and mugs of tea from Beetle, licks and cuddles from Sjambok and Jaffa, and the knowledge that there were still nineteen horses who needed me to see to their every need, got me through it.

The next day it was business as usual.

Chapter Twenty-six
Whose Idea Was This?

Winters could be hard at Blue Well. The people we'd bought it from told tales of trying to walk across that windy moorland in snowy weather and tripping over the tops of telegraph poles, buried in the drifts. I suspected it might be a bit of a tall tale. Until we had our first bad winter.

It wasn't so much the quantity of snow which fell. It was the relentless wind, cutting through a body like a knife through butter and piling up the drifts to incredible heights. A big snow plough with a blower on would try to keep the road clear because of the forestry lorries and the milk tankers needing to get through. One memorable day, even that became wedged solid in a drift and Simon and I had to go and give them a hand to dig it out.

The day I stopped being able to get out in the 4 x 4 pick-up which had replaced the Renault 5, I had to acknowledge that the tales were probably true. Even if I got a grip with the tyres, the drifts were so deep there was no way through them,

Added to that, I had no water. I had taken the precaution of leaving the kitchen tap on a slow trickle overnight to stop things from freezing up. Never having experienced anything like it before, however, I had completely under-estimated the wind chill factor. I went into the kitchen first thing, looking forward to my morning cup of tea before starting the round of feeding the animals, to be greeted by a stalactite of solid ice between the tap and the sink. The water was frozen up solid. It stayed like that for three weeks, too.

My mother had always had a siege mentality. Ever since we had heavy snowfall in England in the 1960s which made it hard to get to the shops, the spare cupboard upstairs had always been stuffed full of essentials. Enough tea bags to host a royal garden party, sugar, powdered milk, instant coffee – although none of us drank it – biscuits, tins of meat, fish, fruit and vegetables, the works.

When I knew I was going to be living up a Welsh mountain, often on my own, with not always much time to go shopping, I followed her example. There were plenty of cupboards in the big kitchen and they were always stocked with anything and everything I might need to survive on, should it be necessary. These days it's trendy to be prepared for the Apocalypse and people like me are known as 'Preppers'.

It was the same with food, hay and bedding for the horses, of course, since the business's livelihood depended on their welfare. The immediate concern was the lack of water. I didn't mind washing in heated up snow-melt, and using it to flush the loo. But the average horse drinks between five and ten gallons of water a day, which is at least two big stable buckets' full. And that's an awful lot of water to carry from the stream a hundred yards or so from the property, by myself.

The solution was simple. Put extra rugs on the horses, open their stable doors and the top gate to the moor, spread the hay out there, as it was close to where it was stored, and let them look after themselves. They were no fools. They could easily find their own water. They were warmer moving about and they knew where the best shelter was, even when they chose not to bother with their stables. It always surprised me how much they preferred to be out and mooching round, even in weather I thought would not appeal to them.

As the days went by and I was still marooned, there was a more pressing need. The first bookings for the residential holidays may well be arriving in the post which was not being delivered. I decided to try a foray down to the village of Llanllwni, a couple of miles away, which was where our post ended up if it couldn't be delivered for any reason.

I chose Khassan, the Arab, for the trip. He was surprisingly sensible. He was also powerful. Having been bred to flounder through the sand dunes of the desert, I thought he might be up to tackling the deep drifts.

I smeared Vaseline on the underside of his feet to stop the snow from balling up too badly, filled the saddle bags with emergency provisions just in case, and off we set. It was eye-wateringly cold but I was well wrapped up and Khassan had a thick winter coat.

I knew the home moor well and horses have an amazing sense of direction. I thought between us we could find our way across the desolate white landscape with no trouble. Some of the tracks we usually rode on were nothing but narrow, single-file sheep tracks, but familiar to both of us.

Just one step out of line and down we both plummeted into a deep, cold drift. Khassan was still upright, and I was still in the saddle, somehow. But the snow came almost up to my waist and only his head, with a rather surprised expression on his face, was poking out.

We looked at one another for a moment and it was clear what my mount thought of my mad idea of venturing out. By unspoken mutual agreement, once we'd struggled clear of the drift, we went back home again and didn't venture out until the 4x4 could be brought back into play.

After that experience, I decided that for future winters I would keep as few horses at home as possible. The rest would be put out on loan to approved homes. It made financial sense for one thing. It cost a lot to keep them through potentially long months when they wouldn't be earning. I'd keep a couple I could ride, plus any liveries I had in. The rest could pack up their teddy bears and go off on holiday until the better weather came and the centre was once more in full swing.

I was still anxious to be earning my own source of independent income whenever I could, which is why, out of season, I took what work I could find. I got some hours teaching on the equine courses at the college where Jill worked. Quite by chance, I also got some work providing horses for film and television work.

A man phoned up one day saying he was temporarily working in the area and wanted to do a bit of riding. He admitted to being a complete novice. Accepting his limitations was always a good opener. I agreed to start him with a couple of lessons then, if he was safe enough, I could put him on something reliable to take him out hacking, which was what he really wanted to do.

Chieftain, the big tank, was always a safe bet. He'd successfully taught Marty and Alex to ride, as well as many others. He was basically an idle lump who would never do anything scary as it involved using too much energy.

One day as we were out hacking together, the man, Steve, told me he worked in films and television as a location finder. It was his job to seek out the best places to film bits of the current project. He'd also been charged, on this occasion, with sourcing some horses for a period drama being made for the Welsh TV channel, S4C.

It was based on a true story and involved a manhunt, with a determined policeman on the trail of someone who had killed a gamekeeper. They needed Welsh cobs, to be in keeping with the setting. In particular, they need a striking one for the policeman to ride. It needed to be a signature horse, something that as soon as the viewers saw it, they would know it was the bobby, hot on the trail of the killer.

As it happened, I had the perfect horse. Visually, that was. Lloyd was a jet-black cob, old-fashioned type, all long flowing mane and tail, with lots of feathering on his legs. The problem might be that he was definitely not a novice ride, being decidedly lively. He was fine for anyone who could ride, though.

I'd gone to see him, with his potential new owner, and the viewing hadn't gone all that well. The man who was selling him said he'd ride him first to show off his paces. He climbed on board, jogged down to the end of his driveway and disappeared round the corner.

The next thing was Lloyd, returning riderless at full tilt, wild black hair streaming in the breeze of his passing as he galloped back towards his stable. His owner came running along behind calling to him as if he were a gun-dog who might come back to his master's whistle.

I rode him next and found that, the minute he tried the same trick with me - a drop of the shoulder, a spin on the hocks - a firm hand on the reins and a bit of leg to keep him going forward was all that was really needed to control him. That was confirmed by his soon-to-be new owner when she rode him.

I told Steve about him, pointed him out on the moor, where he was pronounced ideal. But I stressed again that he was not suitable for a novice. He assured me that the actor who would be riding him was competent and knew how to ride. It said so on his Equity listing.

Up to this point, I hadn't worked with actors. I didn't know, therefore, the lengths to which they will go, and the untruths they will tell, to get a part they want. I was always safety conscious but anyone who could actually ride would have no problems with Lloyd. He was just inclined to take the pee with people who couldn't.

It was agreed that I would supply three horses for three to four days of filming at various locations including picturesque Cenarth Falls.

I was not going to be able to be present myself for the first day's filming as I had lecturing commitments at college. But there should be no problem. I was by now living with a man called Roger. Another much older man. There was nothing of fiery passion about this relationship though. It was more about comfortable companionship.

He made a living driving a horsebox and was very good at it. He and I had made a trip together over to Holland and Germany to deliver some Welsh cobs for breeding. Nice ones. Three young stallions, two mares and two foals. Roger did the driving, I was there to help with the language as he spoke nothing but English.

It was an eventful journey, dealing with all the paperwork, but a successful one. I had been most impressed by Roger's driving skills as he successfully and calmly reversed his big lorry through such a narrow arched entry into one stable-yard that I swear there was only a couple of inches clearance each side and above.

We'd first got to know one another at a briefing for jump judges for a local hunter trial in which I often competed, but on this occasion I would be judging instead. A jump judge sits next to a particular fence, notes the number of each rider who goes past, plus any faults they incur, then hands their sheets over to a runner, usually a Pony Club child on a hairy little mount, to be taken in and added up for scoring.

My notorious sense of humour often gets me noticed, and it did on this occasion. The woman marshalling us judges for the briefing was flapping like a mother hen to find herself one person short. She kept asking, 'Mrs Smith? Where's Mrs Smith?' then, 'Does anyone know who Mrs Smith is?'

I couldn't resist.

'I do,' I said helpfully. 'She's Mr Smith's wife.'

All right, it wasn't that funny, but it certainly tickled Roger, enough to ask me out for a drink. He was a nice man, not the sharpest knife in the drawer, but we got together for a time.

Above all, I trusted him completely transporting my horses, so while I got ready for college, he went on his way carrying Lloyd, another big cob, Missy, who was safe as houses but not dramatic-looking and rather sedate, and Gloss, who was anyone's ride.

Roger was much later home than I expected and looked bone-weary. The way he fell on his bottle of Scotch told me that the day hadn't been a good one.

Roger, bless him, was incapable of telling any story concisely. On the way back from our trip together to the continent he had caused a poor customs officer's eyes to glaze over while he explained, in minute detail, why we might just be a bottle or two of wine over the allowance at the time. He had to go into every minute detail of everything, including the way, in Wales, people are often known by their first name and the name of their property, rather than their surname.

'Well, yes, we might have more wine than we should. We've been to Germany for Peter Pantydderwen. Well, I call him Pantydderwen but it's not his name, of course, it's the name of his farm. So he asked us to take some horses over for him. Well, I say horses, it was three stallions, two mares and two foals. I say stallions, but two of them are only colts really ...' and on and on.

It was late in the evening and an already weary customs officer, after listening to about five minutes of this, non-stop, waved us through with a, 'That's fine, sir, on you go, have a good journey.'

I'll spare you Roger's version of what happened and give you an abridged one instead. Otherwise this book by end up being as long as War and Peace. He arrived at the location to be met by someone from props who offered to ride one of the horses from the lorry to where filming was taking place, if Roger could lead the other two. Roger, quite reasonably, assumed that someone offering to ride probably could do so, but he took the precaution of giving him Missy who was as safe and steady as an armchair, while he led Lloyd and Gloss.

Unfortunately, Mr Prop-man clearly couldn't ride at all. Going down the first slope, Missy broke into a smooth, sedate jog and he just plopped off. Missy cantered away, Lloyd leapt in the air, broke his reins and raced after her.

Chaos ensued and it was not over yet. Once the miscreants were rounded up and the bridle fixed, the 'I can ride really well' actor got on Lloyd. Roger could see he was trembling and he asked to be led down to his starting place for when the director called 'Action!'

The director wanted a dramatic scene where the policeman came galloping up a hill with his cloak flying behind him. Lloyd galloped all right and the actor must have stayed on board for all of about eight seconds, by Roger's reckoning. But he could clearly ride no more than Prop-man and did a spectacular backward roll off the rear end.

End of filming for the day, leaving a furious director with no film taken. Roger was ordered to return the following day with something safe enough for the actor to ride.

I went with him the next day. The first assistant director met us and warned us that the director was still fuming. I offered to have a word with him, not being unduly intimidated by anyone, certainly not by snippy television directors.

As soon as he saw me and went into rant mode, I interrupted him quietly.

'Tell me, if your actor had said he could fly a helicopter and he crashed it, who would you be blaming for that?'

He had the grace to look chastened. He got his galloping scenes, but we used safe and sensible Barney. He was quite striking, with his broad white face and one wall eye. In the fast scenes, it was me in the policeman's uniform on his back. Whenever the actor was on board, I was crouching down out of sight, holding onto Barney for him, so he felt safe.

Chapter Twenty-seven
Show Must Go On

The screen work was reasonably lucrative. I could charge what I liked, pretty much, so I costed it out on an hourly basis for what the horses could have been earning on rides instead, and charged for transport plus waiting time. On any kind of film or TV set, I soon discovered during the course of our now three days' work, there was a lot of waiting time.

I also got some understanding of why people involved in films could sometimes be demanding. I learned how, if your presence was vital to a particular scene, literally anything and everything would be done to ensure you could continue.

One time the director wanted the three horses to be tied up by the reins after the policemen-actors had jogged sedately into shot. I pointed out that horses were not tied up by the reins, except in the westerns, and if they pulled back and broke bridles, that would end filming for the day and I didn't have spares for all three of them.

Could I, therefore, kindly crouch down behind the wall and hold onto the reins it they were tossed over the wall in a show of tying them? I could, normally, I said, but I was unfortunately just about to be struck down with one of my old friends, a migraine. Such a flurry of directions, to ensure that the show could go on. Gophers were dispatched to fetch me, in no particular orders, a chair, several cups of tea, some aspirin, a bacon and mushroom roll and various other items, not all of them of any practical use in the circumstances. We managed – the show went on.

After the initial problems on the first day, once I was there in person and had showed the director I could work professionally, it all became quite good fun. The poor actor was still terrified after his fall on the first day. But transferring him to steady Barney had restored some of his confidence. I also spent some time training Barney in exactly what he had to do before putting the actor on board.

All of my horses were trained to work off the voice. It was a great way of controlling rides when excited children were wanting to push them on faster than was safe. They knew things like 'Trot on!' and more importantly, they knew 'Whoa, stand.'

Barney had to do a scene where he trundled sedately into camera-shot then stopped at a specific point and stood still so his rider could have a conversation with an actor playing a clockmaker, driving a horse and cart. The second actor was a minor Welsh celebrity as he was also something of a rock star. He was nice to work with. I did a scene with him when I doubled for the actor who couldn't ride.

The director wanted at least one action shot of Barney galloping full steam ahead, with me on his back in billowing cloak and a helmet which kept slipping down over my eyes. Barney was not big on galloping but I'd put my spurs on, well hidden by the over-long trousers, and prodded him into a lively lope.

One of the assistant directors told me to gallop him as fast as possible as far as the second tree, pointing off into the distance. I'm short-sighted. I've worn glasses since I was about eleven. Obviously I'd had to remove them as presumably not many Victorian policemen wore glasses at all, let alone the funky purple-rimmed ones I had at the time. I had to confess to not being able to see the first tree, never mind the second. They told me to keep galloping until I heard someone shout for me to stop.

Provoked out of his usual plodding mode, Barney did a respectably fast canter, with a couple of little back-humping bucks of protest. I pulled up when I heard the shout. Then I walked Barney over to the horse and cart, handed over a wanted poster to the rock star, had a little simulated confab, and it was a wrap on the first take.

Back to the changing room we went to get ready for the next scene when the main actor, having got his uniform back from me, would be doing some close-ups with the rock star for a scene later in the storyline. It was all very matey, just one large Portakabin in which to change, shared by everyone.

I was stripping my kit off while the rock star was adjusting his. Then he looked at me and asked if I'd had my gloves on while doing the scene with him. Whoops! I had, and the main actor hadn't in the scene just before, in close-up, before I doubled for him.

We should have come clean to the director, in case he wanted to re-shoot it. But it was cold out there. We'd both come in freezing and shivering and didn't relish the prospect of doing it again. The rock star suggested we keep quiet and wait to see if anyone from continuity picked it up.

Next I had to go and do my Barney-training to get him to stand at exactly the right point, where I placed a white stone for him as a marker. He was as good as gold. He jogged gently up to his stone with the actor on board and stood stock still while the close up scenes were shot. He quickly picked up the idea that he was meant to stand still until someone shouted 'Action!' then he would move in response to a nudge from the rider's legs.

When we got back to Blue Well after a successful day's filming, Roger was about to get Barney off the lorry first. Barney was usually eager to unload so he could go and get his nice full net of hay. But he planted his feet at the top of the ramp and refused to move, despite Roger's best efforts.

Finally the penny dropped. I said, 'Action!' and Barney immediately walked calmly down the ramp. Actors, eh? Give a horse an Equity card and you make a rod for your own back.

About a mile down the road from Blue Well there lived a film director of some note. He'd recently had a minor success with a film about Northern Ireland. I was introduced to him by a friend. The director invited me to visit his house one evening for a drink. I didn't know much about him but I was intrigued to find out, so I went.

When I arrived, he asked me if I'd like something to eat. My strange sixth sense comes in handy sometimes. I declined, saying I'd already eaten, which wasn't entirely true, but said it was fine if he hadn't and wanted to eat something.

He was clearly, as a good friend would say, as mad as cheese. His conversation was rapid and kept flying off in different directions. He was clearly highly intelligent, just extremely eccentric. I watched in fascination as he ate first a large bowl of muesli, then a tin of baked beans, cold, straight from the can, then a big bowl of spaghetti. Just boiled spaghetti on its own, with no dressing, or cheese or anything.

All the time he was sitting in an armchair, a leg hanging over the arm. Once he'd finished his curious meal, he spent some time farting and attempting to set the ensuing gas a-flame with a cigarette lighter.

It was certainly an intriguing and unusual way to spend an evening. I wasn't tempted to repeat the experience. It did, however, lead to some more film work for some of the Blue Well horses.

The director was working on a new film which was going to look at Welsh social history through the eyes of an old woman. And that inevitably meant coal mining. He wanted a scene which was supposed to represent retired pit ponies, grazing on moorland, and he had chosen the home moor outside Blue Well to film it.

I was asked to provide some ponies who would graze in the

background. I couldn't guarantee they would all stay in exactly the required spot for the length of time required. Left to their own devices, horses cover quite a distance when they graze. I had to resort to pouring buckets full of oats into the grass at the spot where they were meant to be hanging around.

I tried to enlist Aslan but he was clearly disgusted at the idea of being a former pit pony, seeing himself more as a show jumper. He kept cantering off, out of camera shot.

One of the loan ponies was a natural, though. He was called Brân, named after a king, a giant, in Welsh mythology. He was a Welsh Section C, a Welsh pony of cob type, a chunky-monkey who was a great favourite for the children's holidays. He was a strawberry roan, a striking pinkish colour.

He managed a scene-stealing piece to camera, which was left in the final film. Two of the characters were discussing the old myth that pit ponies went blind underground. There's no evidence that it was true, although they might well have needed some time to adjust to coming back out into the sunlight.

Brân turned and looked straight into the camera as they were speaking, with an expression which could only have been saying, 'Seriously? You don't believe that old rubbish do you?'

The riding holiday season tended to centre around the Easter holidays, Whitsun and the school summer holidays. The Welsh weather was always uncertain and our exposed situation on top of a plateau meant that whatever the weather was doing, it was extreme up there. When it was hot, the heat was pitiless, with no shade. Rain tended to often be horizontal with the high winds and could find its way through the smallest gap in even purpose-made waterproof clothing.

Nothing was more annoying, after a long ride out in foul weather, than punters (customers) complaining how wet they were. As if somehow I rode along in a protective bubble so that I didn't really have a cold trickle down the back of my neck nor a couple of inches of cold water in the bottom of my riding boots.

But it was always a case of putting on a public face in the teeth of adversity. Show must go on. One of the big problems with taking rides out with people you didn't know and didn't have long to assess was that they would frequently be economical with the truth not just about their riding ability but also about their level of fitness.

The day rides we did were between five and six hours, and that's a lot of riding for people who don't do much of it and aren't really fit. It was never long before some of them would be asking to be allowed to dismount to stretch their legs.

The golden rule was always to allow riders to get off and walk downhill, but never uphill. If they had to do any climbing, they would tire themselves out more quickly and be nothing but a heavy burden for their horse for the rest of the ride.

Allowing one lot of riders to dismount was to result in a neck injury which has left me with two ruptured discs that still give me problems, twenty-five years on. The damage was so impressive that when I was referred for physio here in France, the physiotherapist, or physioterrorist, as I prefer, looked at my X-rays and exclaimed, 'Oh, qu'elle est belle!' What a beauty!

I'd let the riders dismount for a nice long walk down a hill, then asked them to get back up to go up the other side of the valley. One was struggling to get back on, so I helpfully leaned forward from my horse to hold hers still for her. She was still having difficulty and in her efforts, she managed to back-elbow my mount, George, on the nose. He flung his head back and caught me right on the forehead, hyper-extending my neck to the extent that I heard all sorts of nasty crunching and tearing noises.

What could I do? We were still an hour's ride from home, with no mobile phones and no means of summoning aid. I just had to grit my teeth against the pain and get the punters back as safely as I could, without letting them see I was injured.

The full impact of the damage didn't manifest itself until the following day when I was totally unable to get out of bed, without pulling my head up off the pillow by the hair. Luckily, one of the helpers at the time could drive and carted me off to the nearest hospital casualty department. X-rays showed a couple of impressive chip fractures and there was also a lot of soft tissue damage, including torn ligaments.

A month in a neck collar, painkillers, restricted duties and a lot of frustration before it was back in the saddle and getting on with the work. That was both at Blue Well and doing whatever other bits I could to have some pocket money, as I was still not drawing any salary from the business.

One of the jobs I did was working as a case tracker for the newly-created Crown Prosecution Service. In the days before computers, every piece of relevant paperwork for each individual case had to be collated and logged by hand to ensure the right file got to the right court on the right date. Not as easy as it sounds in a country where seemingly those of the population not called Jones are called Williams, Davies or Evans.

It was fascinating and I loved it. I was offered the opportunity to stay on and train as a legal executive. But the call of the horses was too strong and I declined. What I learned has proved of great help to me latterly as a writer of crime fiction.

I wasn't through with the injuries yet, though. Jill's horse Pearl had a nasty surprise up her sleeve for me.

Pearl and I generally got on well. I sometimes competed on her if Jill wasn't doing so, and I often rode her when Jill was at work, to keep her fit. I'd been riding her with others when one rider had a fall and broke a collar bone. The ambulance couldn't get all that close so I finished up having to carry a cylinder of Entonox painkilling gas across the more to the stricken faller. Not the safest thing to do on horseback. I knew I could trust Pearl to be sensible, though.

On another occasion during a rather adventurous exploring ride, she might just have saved my life. I was at the front, trail-blazing as usual. The ground was much boggier than I'd appreciated and she and I fell into some scarily sucking swamp-like stuff. The way we fell, my foot was stuck underneath her, trapped in the stirrup.

When she struggled to her feet, it was still caught fast. More in hope than anticipation, I instructed her to 'Whoa, stand.' Fortunately, she did, like a rock, while I somehow managed to right myself and free my foot. Had she taken flight at that moment, I could potentially have been dragged and killed, or at least seriously injured.

For reasons best known to herself, Pearl hated my by now ex-sister-in-law Debs. It was so bad that if I was in the stable grooming Pearl and she heard Debs' car coming down the drive, she would start lashing out in anger, knocking chunks out of the kick-boards in her loose box.

One day Debs kindly went into the field to bring in some horses for me, Pearl included. A part of the ground was boggy and Debs' wellies got stuck in the mud. With careful precision and malice aforethought, Pearl, seeing her plight, walked up to her and calmly kicked her right on the kneecap while she was immobilised, which put her in plaster for several weeks.

Pearl was sometimes a bit funny about going into her stable. I was just closing the door behind her on one occasion when she changed her mind about going in and shoulder-charged the door, just as I was standing squarely in front of it about to shut the bolts.

The effect should have been to flip me to the side, out of harm's way. Unfortunately, the bottom of the door went over the top of one of my feet so, immobilised as I was, I was flung backwards down the concrete ramp to land on the back of my head.

My brother was staying with me at the time. His health had taken a nose-dive with the break-up of his marriage and he'd had to return home from the European Commission. I was trying to keep a bit of an eye on him.

He was some distance away, in the kitchen, and has always sworn that he heard the thwack as my skull made contact with the ground. I certainly heard my brain sloshing about inside it.

He was highly trained in first aid so he rushed to my side and told me to lie perfectly still as I had hit my head and mustn't move.

As is often the way, the superficial injury to my foot was hurting far more than my head so I kept repeating, 'My foot, my foot,' to which he kept replying patiently, 'No, it's your head you've hurt. Do you know where you are? What day is it?'

I was lying head down on a cold concrete slope. It was raining hard and the water was going up my nose in that position. Whether or not I had a serious head injury, I was in danger of drowning if I carried on lying there. I swore at him sufficiently to convince him he could safely allow me to get up and take myself in out of the rain.

I had a thunderous headache for a day or so and my words had a habit of coming out in rather a strange order for about a week. But I survived. It was a case of having to. As soon as I could squash a riding hat on over the impressive lump on the back of my head, I was back taking rides out.

Chapter Twenty-eight
A Tragic Incident

Warning: this is a chapter which involves a tragic incident which some readers may find distressing. I have tried to write it as sensitively as I could.

I was woken one morning, earlier even than my usual starting time for feeding the horses, by a frantic knocking on the front door. A man's voice was shouting something I couldn't quite catch in my still sleep-befuddled state, although I could detect the urgent note.

I was sleeping alone in the upstairs bedroom of the main house. Roger and I had drifted apart. Mere companionship had not proved a strong enough tie to bind us. Besides, he was into an altogether different type of bondage which was not my thing at all.

The salvo on the door and the shouting were continuing so I rolled out of bed, trying to grab something with which to cover myself as I slept as nature intended. Since I had no idea who the person was or what they wanted from me, I had no intention of going down to open the front door.

Instead, I knelt down by the small, low-down window which overlooked the cottage entrance, opened it and stuck my head out, hoping that with the angle, that would be all he could see of me. I hadn't managed to find my glasses so I peered out myopically with still no idea who the dawn visitor was or what he wanted.

I tried to make sense of what he was saying. Something about a horse trapped in a cattle grid. On the Llanllwni road.

Oh dear god no.

I shouted my thanks, grabbing the nearest clothes to hand, pulling them on inside out, back to front - who knew or cared - in my haste. Fumbling and feeling for my glasses, half-falling down the narrow twisty staircase to jump into my wellies.

Think. Think! What to do for best?

Phone the vet. First of all, get a vet there. Before even going to do an assessment. No mobile phones, remember, and the incident was half a mile away. No point getting there and discovering there was urgent need of a vet.

I phoned the vet surgery I used regularly. Thank deity! The horse vet I knew best was on duty. He knew me well enough to know that if I said it was urgent, it was. He would be with me as fast as he could, he assured me.

Next, grab a headcollar. Whatever the situation, I was going to need the means to immobilise an injured and probably panicking horse. Then leap into the 4 x 4 and roar up there as fast as I could.

My mind was racing. The Llanllwni cattle grid separated the home moor, where my horses were grazing, from the big moor, where there were horses and ponies belonging to other nearby farms.

I didn't want the injured animal to be anyone's horse. I wanted it all to be some sort of ghastly error or even a sick practical joke.

Above all, I didn't want it to be one of mine.

The pick-up was bouncing and sliding up the track with the speeds I was asking of it. As I drove, I could see some of my horses starting to make their way down from the moor for their breakfast, having heard the truck coming. I was scanning them frantically, trying to work out which, if any of them, was missing.

I raced up to the top of the moor, where a trig point marked the altitude. From there the road started to go down, towards Llanllwni. And it was from there that I got my first clear view of the cattle grid. My heart nearly stopped when I recognised the horse trapped by the legs in those vicious metal bars.

Chieftain. My big, stubborn old tank. Fighting for his life.

My heart was now beating far faster than it should do. My mouth was dry. My stomach turned over. I wanted to scream, to cry and to be sick, in no particular order.

I drove as near as I dared without frightening him any more, then jumped out with the headcollar. When handling horses, the Germans make a strange noise which I'd learned and used, somewhere between a purr and a trill which has a remarkably calming effect. I used it now as I approached Chieftain, quietly repeating, 'Prrrrrt. Whoa, stand, Chief, good boy.'

A horse is a flight animal. It's only form of self-defence is to run away. If it's prevented from doing so, adrenalin will flood its body to give it the strength to try to do so. Only when the body's system recognises that flight is impossible and death is inevitable will it reach the peaceful state induced by the endorphins finally winning against the adrenalin.

Chieftain was a long way from that blessed peace.

I slipped the headcollar on him and pulled his big head close to my chest, rubbing his ears, stroking that stubborn Roman nose, promising him over and over that it was going to be all right. I was going to get him out.

I had no idea how.

Cattle grids are a device designed to discourage animals from straying. They consist of a shallow pit set into the tarmac with steel joists laid across it. Cars can pass over without pausing. They're considered more practical since drivers don't have to stop to open a gate, with the inherent risk of them not bothering to close it after their passage.

Because of the angle at which a horse places its feet, toe

first, it was possible for a foot to slip down between the bars. But any attempt to withdraw it was thwarted because the bulbs of the heel, and the back of a shoe if the horse was shod, would catch against the T-shaped bars.

Goodness knows what had possessed Chieftain to try to cross it but all four of his big feet had slipped down between the bars. He was stuck fast. His struggles had opened a lot of nasty-looking wounds on his legs and there was a lot of blood.

But Peter the Vet was on his way and I had complete faith in him. He would make it all right. Everything was going to be all right. And as soon as Peter came to take over, I could whiz down to the house to phone 999 for a fire appliance with the tools to cut Chieftain free.

I currently had a young French student helping out, sleeping in the chalet. I could tell him briefly what the situation was and he could start feeding and seeing to the other horses in my absence.

I'd never been more pleased to see Peter in my life. His first priority was to sedate Chieftain to stop him from struggling any more and making his injuries worse. It would take all his considerable skill to get the dose right. He needed to heavily sedate him, as far as he could without knocking him off his feet. If he should fall over onto his side, he risked breaking his legs. He'd already clearly fallen to his knees a few times as he had at least one broken front tooth where his head had hit the ground.

It seemed to take forever for the fire appliance to arrive after I phoned them. They came on blue lights but no siren, knowing they were attending an incident involving livestock, for which they would be specially trained, operating in a rural area.

They had oxyacetylene tools, used for cutting road accident victims out of their vehicles and they got to work with those immediately, with Peter keeping a close level on Chief's levels of sedation. I was still holding and stroking him, putting a hand over his eye to shield from him as much as possible of what was going on. There were sparks flying up as the fire crew worked.

The senior fire officer quickly decided that the cutting tools were not up to the job and they were going to need hydraulic spreaders to force the bars apart. They didn't have any on their vehicle, so he radioed for an urgent despatch of a second appliance which was equipped with them.

It seemed to take hours for it to arrive. We were all powerless in the meantime although the firemen kept battling on. At least Chieftain was now calm and sleepy, standing patiently, his head drooping against me, all fight having been driven from his system by the effects of the tranquillisers.

But at last the second tender arrived, the spreaders were deployed and the big steel bars were bent apart as easily as pulling a paper clip out of shape. The fire crew deployed flat hoses and rigged up a sort of sling underneath Chieftain. Between us all we somehow managed to half lift, half drag him out of the murderous grid from where he tottered under his own steam to the side of the road, with me leading him.

A cheer of relief went up from both fire crews. They'd done it! Finally, against all the odds, they'd got him out. Pleased with themselves, they started rolling up their hoses and putting their equipment away.

But I knew.

I knew before Peter vet started his thorough examination.

I knew before he said anything.

I knew before he turned to me with that look on his face.

Chief's off-hind fetlock, rather like the ankle joint of his back right leg, was shattered beyond repair. Peter had felt and carefully flexed it. Even without the benefit of X-rays, he could tell from the crepitus (the grating sound made by broken bone ends rubbing together) that it was too badly damaged to be viable.

He spoke so kindly and gently. He said because of the

degree of damage and the amount of trauma Chief had already suffered, the best thing was to let him go.

I knew he was right.

Flight animals like horses are hard to immobilise for long periods of time and it can have serious psychological effects on them to try to do so. Especially for a horse like Chief who loved to wander at will.

Wordlessly, trying not to cry in front of everyone, I nodded my agreement and Peter went to get his gun from the car.

The firemen looked absolutely gutted, some of them not understanding at all what was going on. They really thought they'd done it. They thought it had been a successful rescue and there would be a happy ever after ending.

Some of them had clearly never seen a horse being put down before. It's not the gentle slipping away of a beloved dog or cat, nestled in the warm arms of their owner. It's abrupt, seemingly brutal, somewhat primitive. A bolt from a gun through the forehead immediately puts an end to all of the horse's pain and suffering, in an instant. But the body often continues to twitch for a moment, Chief's big feet once more cantering against the tarmac when he fell to his side.

I needn't have worried about hiding my tears. Some of the firemen were wiping their eyes when it was over.

Show must go on. I always said it about running the business. Paint on a smile and see to the punters. But at that moment, I had no idea where I was going to find the strength to smile again.

I was in desperate need of a hug. Alex was away in Devon with his lady-friend. There was no one at Blue Well apart from the French student, affectionately known as Geoffrog. I know he would die of embarrassment if I asked him.

A quick phone call when I got back, to my other mum, Sylve, grandmother of the pony owners, and it was not long before she was coming striding down the driveway, arms outstretched. She was in tears herself. She'd loved Chief almost as much as I had. She folded me to her ample bosom, led me to the kitchen, put the kettle on then hugged and cuddled me some more as she waited for it to boil to make me some tea.

When she had to leave, to see to her own family, I instructed Geoffrog that I was not to be disturbed under any circumstances and crawled back to bed, pulling the covers over my head to shut out the world and all its nastiness.

After I'd cried some more, slept a bit, cried a bit more, it was time to get myself up and into action. The grieving process normally involves an initial period of denial, refusal to believe what has happened. Not for me. It was too indelibly etched on my brain for that. I went straight into the anger phase. White-hot fury, to be precise.

How in the name of anything holy, in a supposedly civilised country, one claiming to be animal-loving to boot, could anything so barbaric happen in the twentieth century? If motorists really couldn't be bothered to get off their bums to open and close gates on common land, then surely there must be some more human way of deterring straying animals.

I decided to do some research. In these days of internet, a quick post on social media, setting up a petition via something like Change.org and within days – possibly even hours – half the world would know all about it. I had to do it the old-fashioned way. I wrote to all the papers and horse magazines I could think of, asking for anyone with similar experiences to contact me.

I thought it might just have been a fluke. One of those things which should never have happened but somehow did and Chief was the poor unlucky horse to draw the short straw. I was horrified by the number of people who contacted me with tragic tales of their own.

Even after my own shocking experience, some of the letters I received were too horrifying even to allude to here. Even more disturbing was the discovery that there were no official records kept of livestock dying as a result of cattle grids. Instead the statistics were all simply lumped together as road traffic accidents.

I started doing some research into alternatives. I'd already seen, on a trip to America with Jill, that some States there simply painted the illusion of a grid on the roads. A clever *trompe-l'œil*, designed to trick the eye into believing it sees something which is not really there. Something like that must surely be economically attractive? Besides which, if any animals did cross it and stray, at least they would be alive.

As part of my research, I also visited every cattle grid in the immediate area to see if they were all built to the same design. One of the big problems with the T-bar shape of the joists was that, inevitably, over time and with constant wear and tear, they became worn down so the edges were sharp.

Then I discovered that over on the far side of the big moor there was one which had round tubes instead of T-shaped joints. Because of its design, it meant that although the gap between the tubes was quite wide at the top, to give the deterrent effect, lower down, at the nine o'clock point on a clockface, they were much closer together.

A horse trying to walk across them would find themselves wobbling and out of balance, which would be likely to cause them to retreat. If they should venture forward, it was much less likely that their feet could slip down far enough to become stuck. Even if that should happen, there were no sharp edges to cut and slice.

I decided to contact at least the local County Council, Dyfed, who were responsible for all highways in the area and therefore for the cattle grids on all the roads. I asked if we could meet to discuss this, with a view to changing Chieftain's grid for one of the round bar design.

Two surveyors came to meet me at the grid. Luckily for me, I had paying guests staying with me at the time, regulars, a nice couple. The husband kindly volunteered to come with me.

It was hard, emotional, to be standing there talking about what had happened. I'm not sure I could have done it alone. I kept hearing the sound of Chieftain's cantering feet.

We all went together to view the round bar grid higher up the mountain, then came back to Chieftain's to discuss the feasibility of changing it. The council agreed to my request and the grid was changed. As far as I know, there has been no serious or fatal accident there since.

At least Chief had not died totally in vain. And his memory lives on. He was one of the horses who used to go to college for the winter months to train the students, and he was very popular. I had a trophy made in his memory which is presented annually to the student having made the best progress on the course.

R.I.P. Chieftain, old friend. You taught a lot of people to ride. You will never be forgotten.

Chapter Twenty-nine
Then One Day

'Blue Well Riding Centre,' I said brightly.

It was how I always answered the phone and it rang often. People enquiring about or booking riding holidays, lessons, hacks. Asking about horses for sale or on loan.

This time there was a pregnant pause. I thought it was possibly an overseas call, or somebody who expected a Welsh speaker to answer. We got a lot of calls from abroad. We'd had unaccompanied children coming on holiday from France, Germany, Spain, even Finland. Then there were all the foreign students who came and worked in the holiday season, either with the horses or in the kitchen.

Then a hesitant voice spoke.

'Hello?'

Another moment of silence.

Then, 'It's me.'

A voice I knew so well. One I never thought I'd hear again. Marty.

In my vivid imagination I'd had him dead of a heart attack, drowned, shot, arrested, in exile, captured by pirates on the high seas.

But here he was. After all those months. It must have been a couple of years or more by now.

I'd never planned for this moment.

I simply said, 'Oh, it's you is it, you little toerag?'

All right, it wasn't brilliant repartee, but the word does mean a contemptible or worthless person and that was pretty much how I'd grown to think of him.

He gave a bitter, ironic laugh.

'Toerag, am I? Believe me, you're better off without me.'

I didn't hang up on him. I probably should have done. But I hate an unsolved mystery and I was genuinely interested it what he had to say for himself. He told me he was phoning up because he knew I read horse magazines and he was going to be featuring in the next edition of one of them.

He said he was now back with his wife and running a trekking centre on a remote island in the Orkneys, with his younger daughter. If he'd said he'd become a Buddhist monk and was living in Tibet I could hardly have been more surprised.

We talked for a bit, awkwardly. I wondered if I would ever have heard from him again had it not been for the magazine article. I also wondered if his wife could have moved him any further away from my clutches if she'd tried. The island was about two miles off the north coast of Scotland. She'd have had to drag him to the northernmost Shetland Islands to put more distance between us.

He kept being interrupted by a small child's voice calling him granddad. Strange, since one of his absences had been to visit the younger daughter who had had to have a termination since she had been exposed to risk from some disease or another, he had told me. Clearly a miracle.

He promised to write to me, then rang off. I wasn't sure if I wanted him to. I think some of the things I had imagined would have been easier to accept than him just lamely trotting off back to the wife and not having the courage to tell me.

For once, he kept his promise and I got a letter from him shortly afterwards. Full of excuses and platitudes. I opened it extremely carefully as I had mischief in mind. I couldn't resist. Once I'd read it, I carefully resealed it and wrote in large letters: 'Not Known At This Address. Return to Sender.'

Exactly as had happened to me with the card I'd sent to the hospital.

A few days later, there was a message on the answerphone. From his wife. Telling me to stop chasing him. It clearly hadn't occurred to her that in order to have returned the letter, he must first have sent it to me.

But this time it really was the end of the Marty saga. Or very nearly.

My brother got wildly excited some months later when there was an article in one of the serious Sunday papers about the hunt for an international arms dealer. He was known as The Rhodesian. Descriptions of him were vague, but all mentioned that he had a Rhodesian accent and the tattoo of a springbok on the left side of his chest.

In hyped Walter Mitty mode, my brother was convinced that the person in the article was Marty. I pointed at that it was not all that unusual for someone from South Africa to have a springbok tattoo as it's the country's national animal. And although Marty was from Rhodesia, he was educated in South Africa.

It was highly unlikely that a wanted arms dealer would agree to appear in a magazine article, especially because an Orkney island was a fairly good place to hide out if you kept your head down, below the radar. But I could never dismiss the thought that it was so soon after that phone call, the first time anyone ever called Blue Well to contact him, that he disappeared.

Then there was the strange case of the arena fence. Although he was strong and fit, Marty was not what I would call a real grafter. He'd do jobs I asked him to and was happy to work alongside me. But he wasn't someone who took the initiative to do things.

He suddenly decided, one day, to construct an arena for me, for schooling horses in. Very useful, especially for backing and schooling young horses. An arena needs a good perimeter fence, of course, and to be substantial, a fence needs strong posts, well set into the ground.

We didn't have a post-hole digger, either a manual one or the use of a tractor-mounted one, so Marty dug them with his bare hands. He dug, and dug, and dug. Then he got down on his side, put his hand down the hole and dug some more. They were certainly deep post-holes. Impressively so.

After that article, I couldn't help but wonder if there was anything down those holes, underneath the posts. I never pulled them up to look. They may still be in place. If there ever was anything there, it might well still be there.

Now that really is the end of the Marty saga. Unless, following our recurring theme of coincidences, someone who happens to be reading this book knows any more.

I was creeping towards the dreaded forty years old. Time for mid-life crises. I'd done the older man. Perhaps it was time to take a toy-boy? Instead, I decided to be boringly sensible and middle-aged and go back to college.

If I ever wanted to take my BHS qualifications any further, it was about time to stop thinking about it and do something constructive. It would be useful for the business as I could do more private teaching. There was always a demand for good instructors, and I already had the good horses as I regularly competed on most of mine.

The college where Jill worked in Carmarthen had a course which combined the BHS Stage IV (Intermediate) exams with the famous Anceybum – Advanced National Certificate in Equine Business management. It was a one year full-time course and it involved several weeks on residential placement at an equestrian centre in Gloucestershire for the riding and stable management elements.

By this time, Alexander Beetle was back in residence and helping out. I knew I could perfectly safely leave him in sole charge of the place when I was away studying. Being a college course, it had the same academic holiday periods as most schools so I could continue to run the business.

I'd stopped taking adults on residential holidays staying at Blue Well. The standard of accommodation that was expected was far higher than we could reasonably provide on site without enormous refurbishment costs. It was much simpler all round to farm out the residential side of things to local B&Bs. Much less work for me, and a lot nicer than having the PGs around the whole time. My dear friend Sylve became one of my accommodation providers.

I could still do children's residential holidays during the college breaks, as well as hacking and instruction at the weekend, to maintain an income for the business. I signed up for the course.

It felt strange being back as a student. Especially as Jill was to be my course tutor. If I was a naughty student, she would be the one who had to tell me off. We were both mature enough, and good enough friends, for it to work out.

We often went on holiday abroad together and always got on. We also had some completely mad adventures together, like the time we decided to try wild camping deep in Brechfa Forest. The weather conspired against us, I got so wet my legs turned blue where the dye from my denim jodhpurs ran, and we couldn't get a fire going for morning tea. Jill went trotting up the driveway of the first cottage we came across, brandishing a Thomas the Tank Engine flask and asking for hot water, saying we had been sleeping in the forest. I bet the man who spoke to her has dined out on the tale ever since.

There were horses at college, including some of mine, and we would have regular lessons there. But the bulk of the serious stuff would be done up in Gloucestershire. In addition we would have instruction in things like Equine Science, Law for Riding Establishments, Business Management, Computer Skills and First Aid.

When we were considered up to standard, we would be put in for the external BHS exams in Instruction, Stable Management and Riding. The Anceybum would be taken at college at the end of the course.

The riding element of the BHS exam was always going to be the hard one for me. I rode and competed at the right level, reasonably successfully. I'm just not the right shape for the BHS's template. I'm round shouldered and always have been, no matter what I do to straighten up. The illusion is exaggerated by having something of a bump on one shoulder-blade. I've no idea when or where I got it. I suspect I may have broken it at some time and soldiered on – as you do. Show must go on.

I wouldn't weep and wail if I didn't get the Riding. It was the Intermediate Teaching Test I really wanted, which was what would interest customers coming for lessons.

When I was away on the Gloucestershire trips, I would be staying at a B&B and was going to be sharing a room with two other students on the same course. Here we go with those coincidences again. One was the niece of the couple from whom we'd bought Blue Well, the one who used to help to run it for them.

We were diligent and studious students, the three of us. We were there to learn and to pass exams, not to muck about. Our evening meal was served early in our digs – it was usually on the table waiting for us when we got home from the stables. After we'd eaten and perhaps watched a bit of the news, it was off up to our room, books open, questioning one another, working on projects.

As part of our training, we were each responsible for looking after a horse. Mine was a big German Warmblood called Wotsit. She was similar to Ali Baba, from our time in Germany, and I enjoyed riding her. She could be lazy but my electric seat helped with that. She had a big stable, to accommodate her size, and she was a filthy pig to muck out.

She also had a particular party trick. No matter how carefully I put on her jute night rug, with blankets underneath when it was cold, and did up the cross-over surcingles, the following morning she would be stark naked, the rug on the floor, the surcingles still fastened. She always managed to do all her droppings on it, too, so it took me ages to get it clean enough to put back on her. None of the modern, easy-wash, secure nylon rugs available now back in those days.

One morning I couldn't even find the rug. I could have sworn Wotsit was smirking at me as I hunted. She'd dug up the bedding in the centre of the box, wriggled out of her nightie as usual, then pawed straw back over it and added a few piles of dung on top for good measure. Got to love an animal with a sense of humour.

I was assessed as being well up to the standard required for the teaching element of the exam early on so I was entered for it at a college in the West Country. It was a region of strange-sounding place-names, like Zeal Monachorum and Stoke Climsland. I booked myself into a B&B for the night before to be sure of being there on time. I have a horror of being late.

The exam was a lengthy one, in several sections. Candidates had to deliver a stable management lesson, give a lunge lesson, teach a private jumping lesson and a private lesson on the flat, including riding the pupil's horse to assess it, and teach a class lesson.

Candidates were randomly put into pairs and would be examined at the same time, using the same arena. Hopefully, each keeping to their own end. The ability to manage this situation carefully and safely formed part of the assessment process.

My pairing was an absolute dream. She was so bad I would have to be spectacularly awful to look worse. Although I was concentrating on what I was doing, I quickly became aware of her because, right from the beginning, she was a liability. When you're sharing an indoor school with another instructor, it's good manners, not just safe practice, to warn them when you're sending your rider their way. My oppo never did.

Because I'm kinder than I'm often given credit for, I tried to help her by warning her in an overly exaggerated manner of my rider encroaching on her territory.

'Just changing the rein across the long diagonal into your half now,' I would say brightly and loudly, with a bit of a nudge-nudge, wink-wink. I'm sure the examiners thought I was strange. The other candidate still didn't catch on.

We were paired again for the class lesson. We would have a small group of four guinea pig riders to teach, usually students or clients from the host riding centre. One of us would teach while the other rode leading file, then we'd swap over when instructed. I rode first.

I'd taught for years so I knew the drill. I'd also had it constantly drummed into me recently as a student. The first important part of any lesson was to assess. Assess, assess and assess again. And teach what was in front of you. You might have the most brilliant lesson plan of all time in your head. But if your guinea pigs weren't up to it, or if the horses were not suitable for whatever reason, you had to rapidly rip it up and revise your plans.

I already knew my oppo was not from the centre we were at, so assessment was even more important. She did none at all. She didn't even try to find out which horses might kick, so needed to be at the rear of the ride. Nor did she take into account that it was a chilly day, the wind blowing a hooley which was bound to make the steadiest of horses a bit friskier than usual.

Without any real time to warm-up and settle down, she wanted me to go forward to canter to the rear of the ride while the rest stayed in walk. I tried giving her an 'are you sure that's wise?' look, to which she was oblivious. I pushed the little horse I was riding on into a canter and we did practically the entire circuit with him bucking and farting which, judging by the noises behind me, set the rest of them off as well.

It didn't improve much, but somehow we managed to finish the ride with no fallers. Then it was my turn to take over. I first sorted out the known kickers, got the riders to take their stirrups up a hole or two for a lighter seat then got them all going. Lots of trotting, lots of circling, getting the horses to settle down before we could even think of doing any work from my lesson plan.

Then out of the corner of my eye, I saw the examiner, clipboard in hand, get up from her seat and come striding out into the middle of the arena to stand next to me. I was, as they say, gobsmacked. An examiner will only stop a lesson during an exam if they consider it to be dangerous. Bearing in mind that the one prior to mine had been near-carnage, I couldn't begin to imagine what heinous crime I had committed to warrant the need for the intervention.

But the examiner was smiling broadly at me.

'Don't worry,' she said, 'You haven't done anything wrong. Far from it. You clearly know what you're doing. But we're running late so I'm stopping you there to pick up a bit of time.'

Phew! What a mean trick. My legs were all wobbly with the relief.

The rest of the exam, for me, went just as well. In those days, results were announced in public at the end of the day. I'd passed all sections. I was more than a little relieved to hear that my oppo had failed just about everything. At least she might get some better training before she tried to take her career any further.

Chapter Thirty
There May be Trouble Ahead

I was still in contact with The Other Half. He came down after Chieftain's death, since it had been his horse, in a supportive gesture. Our relationship was best described as coldly cordial. He'd kindly lent his flat in London when Debs and I had gone on holiday together to Spain and had needed a stopover in town to get an early flight. He was posted to the Ministry of Defence at that time but was away somewhere or another on the night in question.

I paid for my own holidays always taken in Blue Well's quiet season, from what I earned in my other jobs, as I liked to get away occasionally. The Other Half came once to take over the helm at Blue Well while I visited the USA with Jill and he apparently had a bit of a thing with a friend of mine who was in charge of the horse side as he wasn't sufficiently competent. There was certainly dinner out at a good restaurant, my spies informed me, but it may have been no more than that. All a bit strange, though, since she was still at school. But I was hardly in a position to judge anyone else's morals.

I always kept him in the loop with everything, as a courtesy if nothing else, including me going back to college and my time away in Gloucestershire. He wasn't stationed all that far away at the time so he said he'd drive over to see me one evening.

I didn't imagine the visit would bode well.

He drove down to my digs to pick me up and we went out looking for a suitable pub. I was hoping to get something to eat as, because of the timings, I'd missed out on supper. As it turned out, being a Monday evening, none of the pubs we visited was serving food. I had to make do with a bag of crisps.

Once we'd got our drinks, sat down, and done the lip-service formalities, he said he'd met someone.

I told him I was pleased.

They wanted to get married.

I congratulated him and said I hoped they'd be very happy.

He and I would therefore need to get a divorce.

Absolutely no problem. As soon as it could be arranged.

Then there would be the financial settlement.

Hmm. That might be going to be slightly trickier, I sensed.

He'd been paying the mortgage all along, he told me virtuously.

Yes, and I had been running the business without a wage for nearly eight years, often working seven days a week, sometimes fourteen hours or more a day. That must surely equate?

He had a lawyer. I could get a lawyer. Then his lawyer could talk to my lawyer and we could hopefully arrive at some sort of amicable settlement.

I sensed that there may be trouble ahead.

Part of the college course I was doing included learning about the proven beneficial effects of riding on certain disabilities. Some of our time involved helping out at a local branch of the RDA (Riding for the Disabled Association). In addition, we went to the New Forest to spend a few days observing in a Further Education College for special needs students which did all of its teaching through the medium of Horsemastership. Jill drove us down there in our college's minibus and we all stayed at a nearby Youth Hostel.

It was great fun and a wonderful learning experience. We

were all impressed by the college, by the enthusiasm of the students and how some of them visibly changed as soon as they got on a horse. Each student was in charge of a horse or, if their abilities were more limited, they shared responsibility for one with others. There was a strong work ethic about the whole thing.

The centre had been founded by the mother of the current director who was still actively involved and who spoke to us students a few times to explain the ethos and the practicalities. I had quite a chat with her, after the rest of the students had left the room to go and do other things.

I told her how much I'd liked what I'd seen. She said if ever I was looking for a job I should contact them as they could often make a vacancy for the right sort of person to join the team. Presumably I had been judged to be the right sort of person. I filed the suggestion away in the back of my brain under 'Of Interest' and returned to Blue Well.

The divorce, by mutual consent, was going through swimmingly. The financial agreement not so much. The law had changed so there was no longer any sort of apportioning blame when dealing with the finances. It was generally a straight half and half arrangement. It was just my luck that it was happening shortly before the law changed again when I would have been automatically entitled to a half share of his future Army pension, which would be a good one.

Then he stopped paying the mortgage. Apparently his future second wife had two children, at expensive schools. I was glad The Other Half would be getting stepchildren. He'd always wanted children and had married me knowing full well I didn't. I didn't feel as enthusiastic about having to part-fund their education.

Even running the business flat out to capacity, there wasn't enough profit to pay the mortgage through the lean winter months with next to no income. I doubt the bank would have agreed to me taking it on in any case. And if I found a full-time job which would allow me to pay the mortgage, I would then have no time to run Blue Well as a riding centre so there would be no point in having it.

The Other Half was starting to play dirty. He'd got the Brigadier – remember him? Never my biggest fan – to write a letter to say that me not playing the dutiful wife had cramped The Other Half's style when it came to his military career.

I discussed this on a visit to see my uncle The Judge and his wife. He'd been an Army officer himself so I expected him to toe the military party line. Instead he was absolutely horrified. He said no true officer and gentleman would ever stoop so low as to sling mud of that kind.

I'd got myself a rather dry old stick of a solicitor. An old-fashioned sort, not much given to displays of emotion of any kind. When I went to consult him about this latest twist, he read the Brigadier's statement through slowly and methodically. Then he looked at me over his half-moon spectacles and said, in a dry tone, 'Let me see. When you and your husband separated, he held the rank of Major. Seven years have now elapsed with you living apart and he has reached the rank of ... Major. Yes, well, I don't think we need to respond to that in any way.'

I nearly giggled. Only it didn't seem appropriate in his somewhat staid company.

I wasn't asking for any vast sums of money. I've never been all that interested in money. I'm not remotely material. As long as I have a roof of sorts and something to eat, I'm usually happy. I just wanted a fair fifty-fifty split of everything, then move on.

But with the mortgage going unpaid, we were running a very real risk of getting into negative equity on the property, the only real asset. Time to take out the 'Of Interest' file and to make contact with the college in the New Forest.

Was the offer of a future job just empty words or was there one going? No, it wasn't and yes, when would you like to start?

It sounded too good to be true! But it was just the potential lifeline I needed. Even better, they told me that they could find me a property to rent whenever I wanted to move down there. The area was very much still the old feudal system of large farming estates with farm-worker's cottages which often came up for rent.

Was this fate pushing me in a new direction? Was it one I was meant to go in? But it looked as if it was my only choice.

I told The Other Half I was putting Blue Well on the market and heading for Deepest Dorset. Alex would stay on until it was sold to caretake the place to prevent squatters and to keep it in as decent a condition as possible until a buyer was found.

The loan horses would go back. Pearl and a couple of other liveries could stay on, with Alex looking after them. I'd find good homes for the rest of them. I was taking with me the Welsh Cob Missy, whom I had bought, plus the three foals I'd bred from her.

I arranged for all the furniture my parents had bought for me to be shipped down to Dorset. Anything The Other Half and I had bought or acquired jointly I left behind.

Aslan, my great friend and jumping partner, had already been sold. He'd started to have a few problems with the tendons in his front legs doing the amount of work required of him at Blue Well. Friends of mine ran an RDA group and he'd gone there, where he was happily competing in dressage with a blind rider. I'd warned them about his faulty brakes but apparently he was a paragon of virtue in his new lifestyle. If any disabled rider so much as lost their balance by a degree or two, he would immediately stop and wait for them to be safe before continuing. The treacherous little beast, after all the hairy rides he'd given me, bless him.

Once everything was arranged and packed up, it just remained to say a farewell, hopefully not forever, to Alexander Beetle, then to load myself and two dogs into the car to head south. I still had Sjambok the German Shepherd. Jaffa the collie had reached the grand old age of fifteen-and-a-half before her legs had gone and she was no longer able to stand, when she made a last trip to the vets.

I now had my first cross-bred dog, a medium-sized black collie cross called Mady, who was a lively but biddable dog I'd adopted from a nearby sanctuary. The two of them jumped happily into the back of the car and settled down ready for the big road trip.

My brother had kindly offered to come down with me to help me get settled in my new home. I had no idea where I was going to be living, or what it was like. I'd just been told, over the phone, that it had been arranged for me to rent a small thatched cottage, Cat Cottage, with a large garden. It sounded ideal.

I drove slowly up the stony track towards the road, having a last look round at the place I'd lived in for nearly eight years now. There'd been some great times, as well as the tragedies. But now it was time to move on.

I paused at the top of the drive, where it joined the road, to look across one last time towards Pen y Fan and the Brecon Beacons in the distance. Then I turned onto the road and pulled away, heading for the unknown and the next adventure.

Trot on!

The End